# Second Language Learning

## Through Cooperative Learning

**Julie High**

In consultation with Dr. Spencer Kagan

**Kagan**

1160 Calle Cordillera

San Clemente, CA 92673

(949) 369-6310

Fax: (949) 369-6311

1 (800) WEE CO-OP

www.KaganOnline.com

**ISBN: 1-879097-18-4**

# **T**able of Contents

**Structures** **1**
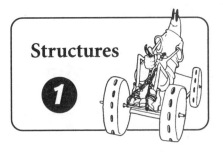

**Social Roles** **2**

**Getting to Know You** **3**

**Making Words Mine** **4**

**Guided Grammar Experiences** **5**

**Writing Skills** **6**

**Lesson Designs** **7**

**8** References & Resources
**9** About the Author

# How To...

**Chapter 3**

## ...Get to Know You

**Chapter 4**

## ...Make Words Mine

**Chapter 5**

## ...Guide Grammar Experiences

**Chapter 6**

## ...Perfect Writing Skills

# Where to Find Structures

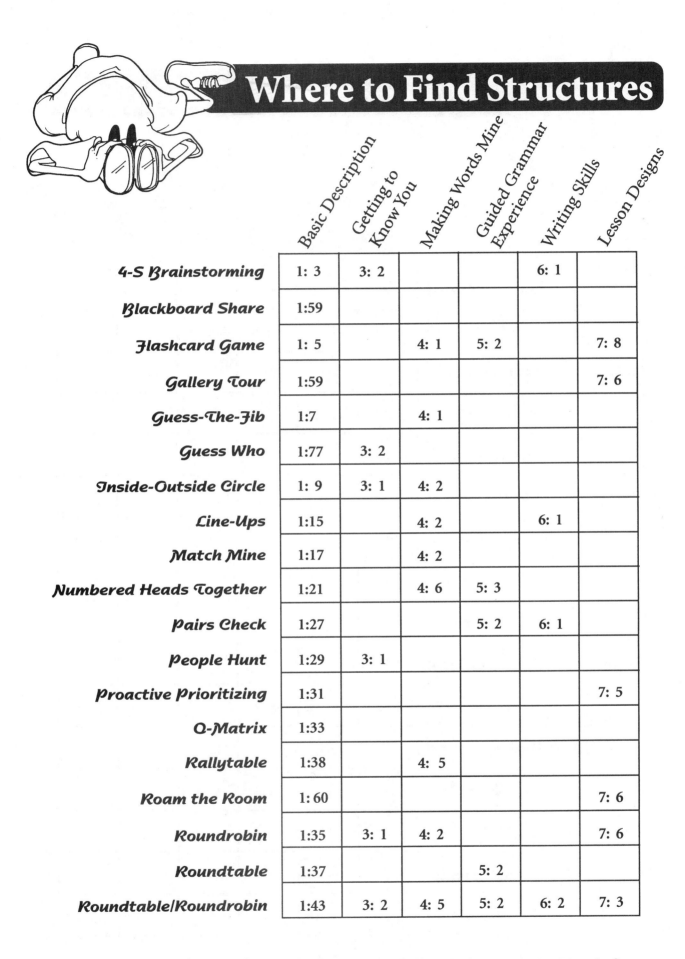

| | Basic Description | Getting to Know You | Making Words Mine | Guided Grammar Experience | Writing Skills | Lesson Designs |
|---|---|---|---|---|---|---|
| **4-S Brainstorming** | 1: 3 | 3: 2 | | | 6: 1 | |
| **Blackboard Share** | 1:59 | | | | | |
| **Flashcard Game** | 1: 5 | | 4: 1 | 5: 2 | | 7: 8 |
| **Gallery Tour** | 1:59 | | | | | 7: 6 |
| **Guess-The-Fib** | 1:7 | | 4: 1 | | | |
| **Guess Who** | 1:77 | 3: 2 | | | | |
| **Inside-Outside Circle** | 1: 9 | 3: 1 | 4: 2 | | | |
| **Line-Ups** | 1:15 | | 4: 2 | | 6: 1 | |
| **Match Mine** | 1:17 | | 4: 2 | | | |
| **Numbered Heads Together** | 1:21 | | 4: 6 | 5: 3 | | |
| **Pairs Check** | 1:27 | | | 5: 2 | 6: 1 | |
| **People Hunt** | 1:29 | 3: 1 | | | | |
| **Proactive Prioritizing** | 1:31 | | | | | 7: 5 |
| **Q-Matrix** | 1:33 | | | | | |
| **Rallytable** | 1:38 | | 4: 5 | | | |
| **Roam the Room** | 1: 60 | | | | | 7: 6 |
| **Roundrobin** | 1:35 | 3: 1 | 4: 2 | | | 7: 6 |
| **Roundtable** | 1:37 | | | 5: 2 | | |
| **Roundtable/Roundrobin** | 1:43 | 3: 2 | 4: 5 | 5: 2 | 6: 2 | 7: 3 |

**Julie High:** *Second Language Learning through Cooperative Learning*©
Publisher: Kagan Cooperative Learning • 1 (800) WEE CO-OP

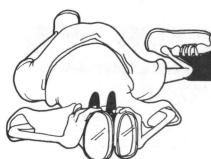

# Where to Find Structures

| | Basic Description | Getting to Know You | Making Words Mine | Guided Grammar Experience | Writing Skills | Lesson Designs |
|---|---|---|---|---|---|---|
| **Same-Different** | 1:47 | | 4: 6 | | | |
| **Send-A-Problem** | 1:53 | | 4: 6 | 5: 3 | | |
| **Simultaneous Roundtable/Roundrobin** | 1:37 | | | | 6: 2 | |
| **Simultaneous Sharing** | 1:59 | | | | | |
| **Spend-A-Buck** | 1:63 | | | | | 7: 3 |
| **Story Scramble** | 1:65 | | | | 6: 3 | |
| **Team Collage** | 1:67 | | 4: 7 | | | 7: 5 |
| **Team Discussion** | 7: 6 | | | | | 7: 6 |
| **Team Draw** | 1:68 | | 4: 7 | | | |
| **Team Inside-Outside Circle** | 1:10 | | | | | |
| **Team Projects** | 1:67 | | 4: 7 | | | 7: 5 |
| **Three-Step Interview** | 1:73 | 3: 3 | | 5: 1 | | |
| **Turn Toss** | 1:75 | 3: 2 | | 5: 3 | | |
| **Two Stay, Two Stray** | 1:60 | | | | | 7: 4 |
| **Where Am I?** | 1:78 | | 4: 7 | | | |
| **Who Am I?** | 1:77 | 3: 3 | | | | |

**Julie High:** *Second Language Learning through Cooperative Learning*©
Publisher: Kagan Cooperative Learning • 1 (800) WEE CO-OP

# Foreword
## by Spencer Kagan

## *Two Needs of a Nation*

Julie High's book appears to be a simple collection of do-tomorrow activities. Her book, however is much more. At root, the book addresses two fundamental needs of any society: The need to educate all of its citizens to the fullest, and the need to optimize relations with other nations. Lack of effective second language acquisition programs in the United States (as well as in other countries) stand squarely in the way of meeting both needs. In the United States, legal and illegal immigration is presenting us with increasing numbers of non-English speaking and very limited English proficient students.

For these immigrants and their children, the activities in Julie's book are essential if they are to become fully productive members of the society. English is the key which opens the door to the rest of the curriculum. Without it, large segments of our population are relegated to a life of unrealized potential.

But Julie's book is not just for our immigrants; it is for the mainstream, fluent English proficient population as well. The world is changing. We are entering the 21st Century. When historians look back at the 21st Century, they will see it as the time when the world of independent nation-states dissolved. Economics and technology are fast creating an interdependent global village in which the knowledge of several languages will be a necessity for the average person wishing to maximize his/her potential. A multilingual population is a necessity, if for no other reason, than for our economic survival in the world of nations.

A multilingual population is not a difficult goal. It only seems like a distant goal to a nation in which almost 90% of the students who pass their foreign language classes never reach true fluency. It seems a difficult goal to a nation which for years has settled on ineffective second language teaching methods. Most of us struggled through our French, or German, or Spanish classes to graduate with more frustration than fluency. So the task of creating a multilingual nation seems forbidding. But consider this: Most small children exposed to a second or even third language will acquire those languages in short order, without exceptional effort. We can easily have a multilingual population if only we apply the same principles of language acquisition children automatically apply when learning their first language. We have failed our students, not because the task is too hard, but because we have approached the task with the wrong tools. We need to turn around our approach to teaching a second language. And the revolution has begun.

## Cooperative Learning and the Language Acquisition Revolution

We are undergoing a transformation in how we teach our students a second language. The traditional methods failed. Yes, we got the students to memorize vocabulary words and conjugations, and to give them back successfully on a weekly test. But no, we never produced fluency in the target language. Why not? Because memorizing conjugations and grammar structures produces at best some *knowledge about a language.* Knowledge about a language is very different from *acquiring the language.*

Think about skiing. Reading books about skiing gives us knowledge about skiing, but books alone do not prepare us to ski steep slopes. Just as we learn to ski by skiing, we learn to speak by speaking. Memorizing grammar rules has little to do with learning to speak fluently in conversation. Fluency in a language is acquired in the repeated process of negotiating meaning in the context of supportive social interactions.

Elizabeth Cohen and her colleagues at Stanford University discovered something quite fascinating while researching the effects of Descubrimiento, a bilingual math/science cooperative learning program. The program provides no direct instruction in English. It does provide math/science experiments for students to conduct, and has students discuss what they are to do before conducting each experiment. Materials are provided in Spanish and English and students are encouraged to negotiate meaning in any language which will foster understanding.

A fascinating discovery in the research occurred when looking at outcomes for students limited in English proficiency. The students, as expected, learned far more about math and science than students who did not participate in the cooperative learning program. The unexpected finding was that in terms of grade-equivalent gains, the students showed greater gains in English language proficiency than in math/science! With no formal language acquisition program, these students were showing remarkable gains in a second language. It turns out that a sure road to language learning is to structure social interaction to maximize the need to communicate in the target language. This communicative approach works far better than having students spend hours in formal instruction in vocabulary and language mechanics.

## Why Cooperative Learning Fosters Language Acquisition?

As simple as the activities in Julie's book appear, they are firmly rooted in language acquisition theory. When we are implementing the cooperative learning activities Julie provides, we are putting into practice five fundamental principles of language acquisition theory.

### 1. Maximizing Language Output: The Simultaneity Principle

We learn to speak by speaking. Students learn to speak in proportion to the extent to which they actually speak the target language. And Cooperative Learning, by implementing the simultaneity principle, maximizes student language production.

In fact, the structure of the traditional classroom is exquisitely designed to *prevent* language learning.

Let's examine for a moment the traditional structure. A teacher asks a question. Students raise their hands. A student is called upon, and responds. Another question is asked. Another student is called upon to respond. The most fundamental aspect of this traditional approach to teaching is that it is a sequential structure. That is, students are called upon to participate one at a time, in sequence. It is as if we had placed all the students in a line, each to wait his/her turn to become an active participant to produce language. With a sequential structure, if we have thirty students for an hour and want to maximize active language output, the very best we can do is to allow each student two minutes to talk. Two minutes per student times thirty students, and the hour is over! Two minutes to express oneself in the target language — and 58 minutes to wait your turn. That ratio of student talk to student listening is exquisitely designed to prevent language acquisition!

In cooperative learning we discard sequential structures for simultaneous structures. Rather than calling on the students to participate one-at-a-time, we direct them to talk to each other in pairs, all students at once. The interaction is simultaneous, occurring all over the room.

Let's contrast the amount of language production possible during the same time frame using a traditional, sequential structure versus a simultaneous structure. Let's say we want to devote thirty minutes of class time to having our class of thirty students practice speaking. In the traditional approach, we call on students one-at-a-time to respond to questions. In thirty minutes, this produces an average student

language production time of less than a minute per student. (Each student gets less than a full minute because it takes some time for the teacher to ask each question, and often to respond as well.) In the cooperative approach during that same half hour, the students are engaged in carefully designed pair discussions and the students produce language for approximately fifteen minutes each! So compared to a traditional approach, a cooperative approach is over fifteen times as efficient in producing language output.

When we use the simple activities described in Julie's book, we are radically increasing the proportion of time students produce language. And because students learn to speak by speaking, we radically increase language learning.

## 2. Moving Toward Meaning: The Communicative Approach

When students answer a question posed by the teacher they are engaging in *display behavior*. They are showing off what they know, speaking to be evaluated. When students are sharing with each other what they did over the weekend they are engaging in *communicative behavior*. During communicative behavior, words are produced not as an end in themselves, but as a means toward accomplishing a goal, communicating meaning. The student in the act of communicating is not offering him/herself up as an object be evaluated. In fact, during true communication, the student forgets him/herself. The focus is on transferring meaning. When words are the means not the ends, words flow. Fluency in a language occurs when the language is used as a vehicle for communication.

During the process of communication, there is negotiation of meaning. The speaker monitors the effect of his/her communication on the listener, and if he/she does not feel understood, adjusts, using a different word or phrase. When communication is achieved, the words or phrases which worked are remembered, stored for future use. The focus is away from the speaker and on the listener. This communicative process is quite in contrast to the self-consciousness focus which occurs when students are called upon to recite in the traditional language classroom. The focus is on whether the language was correct or not.

In the process of negotiating meaning with one or more partners, a number of wonderful things happen. If the communication is to be meaningful to the participants, the speaker needs to communicate and the listeners need to understand. In this exchange of meaning, the communicators help each other. If I do not know a word, my partner supplies one. If my partner does not seem to comprehend my word, I try another. In either case language learning occurs. The communicative process is the opposite of *learning about* the language; it is *living in* the language. We are skiing, not reading books about skiing.

The traditional approach, memorizing rules of grammar and vocabulary words, is a formal approach. The formal approach, used alone, is based on a false assumption that learning words and sentence structures out of context will lead to transfer of those words and structures to the act of speaking. Transfer, though is a difficult process and cannot be assumed. In the flow of a conversation, I do not have time in the middle of a sentence to recall a table of verb conjugations, mentally scan the table, pull out the right verb, plug it into the sentence, and keep talking. Speaking does not wait. Fluency is obtained in a whole different way. It comes from hearing and

understanding phrases correctly modeled and from having the opportunity to apply that learning in the process of negotiating meaning. There is a place in the language classroom for learning vocabulary words and correct grammar. But learning the elements of a language out of context must be no more than one small part of the language experience we provide. It must be complemented by a wide range of student experiences designed to apply that vocabulary and grammar in the context of personally meaningful communication.

Importantly, the cooperative learning structures can be used in both the formal and the communicative aspects of language learning. For example, in Inside-Outside Circle, students may face a partner to hold up a picture prompt to facilitate vocabulary practice (formal instruction), or they may face a partner to talking about a dream vacation (natural, communicative instruction). The trick in facilitating language learning is to have the formal and communicative aspects of the learning complement each other. That is, after students have played Match Mine or the Flashcard Game on food words, they discuss and interact as they plan a delicious meal.

## 3. The Supportive Context: Reducing Risk

Fluency in a language is partially a function of opportunity to speak. It is also partially a function of willingness to speak. Willingness to speak is determined by a simple formula:

**Willingness = Attraction - Fear**

How do we make speaking a foreign language more attractive while reducing the anxiety naturally associated with communicating with unfamiliar words? To a large extent, the answer lies in group size and familiarity. The more listeners, and the less anticipated support from the listeners, the greater the fear. Picture yourself learning a new language. You have learned a few new phrases and it is time to try them out. Your teacher announces that tomorrow you will give a short talk in the target language. As an afterthought she says, "And by the way, your talk will be in the auditorium, which seats 1000 people. We are expecting a full house." Contrast your reaction in that situation with how you would feel if she instead said you will speak only to one other student in the class, and it will be a student you have worked with before and know well. All other things being equal, our fear of speaking decreases with the size and familiarity of the audience.

There is often considerable fear associated with speaking in a second language. Students limited in language proficiency are often unsure of the content so they fear making a mistake. They are also unsure of the language and do not want to risk embarrassment. Stanley Shacter did a series of experiments that established that when individuals are fearful, they seek comfort through affiliation. Getting closer to others reduces fear. If you were in a room with a group of strangers and suddenly a large lion walked in and the door slammed shut, you would find yourself moving closer to the other people in the room. From the time of birth we have an instinct to move closer to others during times of threat; babies make a fearful cry until they are held close. This fear-affiliation link has survival value and is instinctual. So, when we provide supportive cooperative learning groups for our second language students, we are reducing anxiety – often enough to make speaking more comfortable and more likely.

As part of a research project on cooperative learning and language acquisition I spent hours observing limited English proficient students as they participated in different cooperative learning structures. I remember well one of those observation periods in which I followed a limited english proficient boy for an hour through a lesson. During the lesson a range of structures were used. Sometimes the teacher called on students to share with the whole class; other times, the students worked in teams. As the lesson moved on, I became concerned because the boy was mute. He did not speak a word. I did not know if he understood anything of the concept being taught. At the very end of the lesson, the teacher directed students to pair up and summarize what they had learned. She first gave person A in the pair a chance to share for two minutes, and then gave person B a chance. The boy I was following was the B person in his pair. To my great surprise, when it was his turn, he opened up with a flood of language! This same student who was not ready to speak to the whole class, and not even to his own team, was more than ready to share with one other person when he knew it was his turn and he had full attention!

So one of the things we do when we use cooperative teams in our class is create an environment in which it is safer to speak. Sharing with one other you know well is easier than sharing with three, and sharing with teammates is very much easier than giving a talk or presentation to the whole class. Cooperative teams and pairs provide a supportive context which reduces fear, increasing willingness to speak.

## 4. Peers Pulling Language
Language production is a push and pull process. When I need to buy something, share a feeling with a friend, or plan a trip with the family, language production is primarily a push process. That is, energy to

express myself builds up, tending to push language out. On the other hand, when I am asked the time of day, or what I feel about the war in Iraq, or possible topics for our team presentation, language production is primarily a pull process. That is, others around me are pulling language out.

Positive Interdependence is created among students any time one student's performance can be enhanced by the performance of another. For example, if each student reads about a current event, shares his or her current event within their team, and then all students are individually assessed on their knowledge of all the current events, we create positive interdependence. How well any one student does on the quiz can be enhanced by the other three reading and reporting well. Whenever we create positive interdependence among students we create a situation in which language is likely to be pulled from individuals by their peers. If I know I will be assessed on a current event being reported on by a teammate, I will ask questions of the teammate. These questions in turn will pull higher levels of language production and learning from the student.

There are a number of other ways in which peers facilitate language acquisition: They provide a missing word or phrase, they model words and phrases which might not otherwise be heard, and they adjust their level of language difficulty in order to be understood by their teammates, providing comprehensible input. With regard to this last point, the cooperative learning team can do something a teacher cannot. As teachers, we often face a dilemma: When speaking with the whole class, if we speak at a level of difficulty easy enough for the whole class to understand, we fail to provide adequate stimulation for the highest achieving students; on the other hand if we

speak to stimulate our highest students, we lose the lowest students. We cannot provide optimal language experiences for all students at once. Within a pair or team, however, the dilemma is reduced: students can adjust their level of language difficulty to make input more comprehensible for their teammates.

## 5. Language Learning and Gambit Development

Each time I check back on a group of teachers first attempting cooperative learning in their classrooms, I find they are dealing with a similar set of problems. They report excitement, involvement, and enjoyment of cooperative learning among their students. But they have problems because students do not know how to work together well. With all good intentions a high achiever begins to take over a group, and resentments build up in the teammates. Or students give each other put-downs, undermining their future willingness to share or work together. A very successful response to a large number of social skill problems has been the Structured Natural Approach in which students acquire a "Skill-of-the-Week."

The most important aspect of this Structured Natural Approach for language acquisition is gambit development: Students learn what to say and what to do, to work well together. For example, if a Joe begins to dominate a group, the other students learn verbal gambits like, "Susan, I would like to hear your ideas on that." or "Does anyone else on the team have anything to add?" Instead of put-downs, the students learn praising gambits such as, "Great idea!" and "You certainly got that one right!"

This gambit development empowers students to function more effectively in social interactions. At the same time, gambit development is linguistic development. Gambit development is a functional approach to language development; students acquire the phrases which allow them to function, and to accomplish certain goals. As students are given the words which allow them to function socially, they are developing critical language skills.

## *Thanks to Julie*

It is only occasionally that we are given a gift that at once makes teaching easier and more effective. The simple activities Julie describes are easy to implement. And students love them. Teaching becomes more of a joy. As we implement these seemingly simple activities, we are implementing a very sophisticated language acquisition program based on the best of language acquisition theory. Julie, we thank you.

## *Note from the Publisher:*
### *Two Awards for Julie*
With the publication of this book, we at *Kagan Cooperative Learning* present Julie High with two awards:

## Award 1:
### The KCL Perseverence Award
Julie has earned the first *Kagan Cooperative Learning* Author Perseverence Award. I trust that Julie won't mind if I share that she began work on this book seven years ago! At one of our Summer Institutes seven years ago Julie proposed the idea of this book. I was positive and said, "Show me an outline." The next year, she was back to summer training; this time with an outline. I suggested some changes. Guess what? It wasn't until the following year that I heard from Julie again about the book. Julie was back for more training and had made the sug-

gested changes. Unfortunately, in the meantime we had made some fundamental theoretical changes in the Structural Approach to cooperative learning, so I had yet more changes to suggest. And so it went. Julie never complained. Over the years she has oft repeated with a smile, "If it will make it a better book, let's do it." Julie's book was longer by far in preparation than any in the history of our company; it is a contribution whose time has come. Finally.

## Award 2:
### The KCL Good Spirits Award
Working with authors can be touchy, as I am sure any publisher can testify. In the process of putting together a book, the illustrator, the editor, the formatter, the consultants, and the publisher all attempt to make the best book possible — but their experiences can lead them to tug in different directions. An author may feel tired of making changes, or may simply want it their way. Julie is different. Whenever I or others have made a suggestion, Julie is open. Sometimes I have wanted to ask her, "How come you are not like the other authors, ready to defend your work?" But by now I know what she would say: "If it will make it a better book, let's do it." Now, whenever I mention Julie's book with the formatters or, for that matter, anyone on the KCL staff who has had any contact with the project, they just smile. Julie has made the process of putting a book together more pleasant than any of us imagined it could be. Julie wins the KCL Good Spirits Award — hands down.

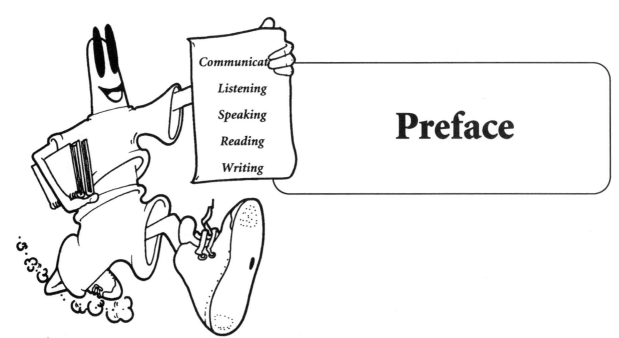

Communicat[...]
Listening
Speaking
Reading
Writing

# Preface

This book is dedicated to the enthusiasm and creativity of the many teachers committed to meeting the challenge of the increasingly diverse student populations in our classrooms. Teachers who hear many different languages in one classroom are on the leading edge of our professional response to the sociocultural evolution presented to us as we approach the twenty-first century. The language teacher is in many ways the luckiest of all because communication and listening, speaking, reading, and writing skills are the underlying goals of every lesson. While acquiring these skills, students can learn more about the world, each other, and themselves and still be meeting the standards of a traditional foreign language curriculum.

As a French, language arts, and ESL teacher for twelve years, I was very inspired by the natural context for communication provided by cooperative learning experiences in the classroom. The transition from a traditional teaching style to creating a cooperative learning environment for my students was accelerated by the enthusiastic response of my students to the opportunities to use and enjoy the second language. This book is a collection of excellent accessible activities that will be a valuable resource for teachers of ESL and other foreign languages.

Many people have assisted me in developing this book. I am very grateful to Dr. Spencer Kagan for encouraging me through every challenge, Celso Rodriguez for his artistic genius, Catherine Hurlbert for her attention to every detail while formatting this book, to Jill Carroll for her editorial input, and most especially, all the hundreds of students who co-created what I share with you now.

I invite you to regard your classroom as your laboratory, and your students as your assistants in discovering increasingly better ways of learning together how to communicate about all things.

*Julie High*

Julie High
April 1993

**Julie High:** *Second Language Learning through Cooperative Learning*©
Publisher: Kagan Cooperative Learning • 1 (800) WEE CO-OP          *XIII*

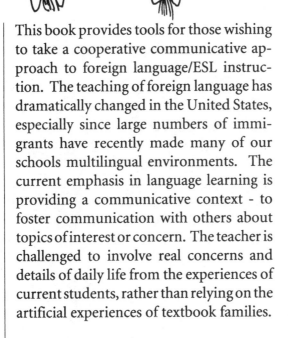

# Foundations:
## Language Learning
## through Cooperative Learning

This book provides tools for those wishing to take a cooperative communicative approach to foreign language/ESL instruction. The teaching of foreign language has dramatically changed in the United States, especially since large numbers of immigrants have recently made many of our schools multilingual environments. The current emphasis in language learning is providing a communicative context - to foster communication with others about topics of interest or concern. The teacher is challenged to involve real concerns and details of daily life from the experiences of current students, rather than relying on the artificial experiences of textbook families.

If the primary goal is communication about important and personal themes, the participation of foreign language students in traditional sequential class activities is inadequate. The application of Spencer Kagan's Structural Approach to Cooperative Learning with its basic principle of simultaneous learning is the most appropriate class activity system to facilitate student opportunity for mastery.

Only when students are given a variety of opportunities to practice listening and speaking with others can they develop mastery with communication tasks. Suppose, for example, that the teacher asks a question in the target language to which most of the students know the answer. When s/he calls on one student in 30 to give the answer, 29 others are actually prevented from responding. Imagine then that instead the teacher asks the same question, gives the students a moment to think, and then has them pair up and share their answers. In this second case, the entire class has the same few seconds to speak that previously were given to only one student. Additionally, the affective filter that prevents many students from risking a wrong answer in front of the whole class is offset, and a student who isn't sure can immediately hear the correct response modeled in the team where s/he can rehearse the answer with little embarrassment.

In a foreign language class, more than in other classes, the true nature of the language arts becomes clear. Listening, speaking, reading and writing are developmental skills that are naturally mastered in sequence. Language learners understand more of what is said to them than they can say in return, and can read with comprehension more than they can write. Writing correctly demonstrates achievement of mastery with the principles of the grammar, vocabulary, and mechanics of language. Because exposure, practice and feedback provide the experiences that increase these skills, then the Structural Approach to Cooperative Learning fosters language acquisition. The structures create additional student involvement and the potential for mastery.

This book is designed to be used by foreign language and English as a Second Language teachers who want to incorporate Cooperative Learning structures into their teaching. It is organized to be a useful quick reference as well as an extensive planning guide for teachers. Activities are organized so that they can be easily integrated into existing lessons. Teachers can try one activity or sequence several in a lesson.

### Chapter 1 — Structures

introduces and describes all the structures referred to in subsequent chapters. The structures are presented in alphabetical order for easy reference, and examples of how to use the structures accompany each.

### Chapter 2 — Roles suggests

taking class time to teach students social skills they will need to succeed in cooperative learning activities. By teaching, modeling, and reinforcing social roles and gambits, we can prepare

students to behave cooperatively in the classroom as well as in the community.

### Chapter 3 — Getting to Know You de-

scribes cooperative learning activities to be used in the introductory phase of every language classroom. The Classbuilding and Teambuilding activities suggested will foster a sense of belonging and begin to reduce student anxiety about taking risks inherent in self-expression.

### Chapter 4 — Making Words Mine rec-

ommends many activities that can structure vocabulary learning cooperatively. Students acquire vocabulary with greater ease when can use it in communicative contexts and have the same words modelled for them by others.

### Chapter 5 — Guided Grammar Experi-

ence suggests many ways to use cooperative learning structures when students are learning to comprehend and apply grammatical conventions.

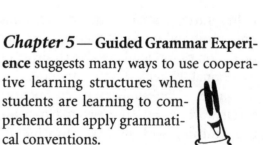

*Chapter 6*—**Writing Skills** detail many activities students can use to develop their ability to express themselves in writing. Student authored materials also provide additional comprehensible text to help other students acquire reading skills.

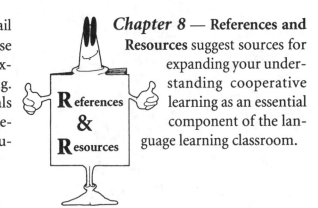

*Chapter 8* — **References and Resources** suggest sources for expanding your understanding cooperative learning as an essential component of the language learning classroom.

*Chapter 7*— **Lesson Designs** invite you to consider extended cooperative learning projects that include several structures and activities leading up to team presentations. Once you and your students are enjoying a variety of cooperative learning structures on a regular basis, you can link several structures together to build to a cumulative project that spans several days of lesson activities.

**Training in Spencer Kagan's Structural Approach is advised to provide the experience with the structures and application to curriculum that create ease and confidence with the activities. Training in the structural approach is widely available. To find out more about trainings, call *Kagan Cooperative Learning* at 1 (800) 933-2667.**

**Rethinking the application of your teaching style and curriculum is always a rewarding challenge. Enjoy!**

# Structures

## Chapter 1

In this chapter we will explore Structures. Structures are the resources that allow teachers to adapt any curriculum experiences cooperatively. They are content free and address the range of involvement and skill development that students need to master a second language. Class activities are built by placing content into a structure. Each time new content is placed into a structure, a new activity is created. For example, 4-S Brainstorming new ways to use a common item would be one activity; 4-S Brainstorming places to go on a vacation is a different activity.

The basic formula in the structural approach is Structure + Content = Activity. In this section of the book, we will focus on the first part of the formula, the structures. In the later chapters, we will see how to insert Language Acquisition content into the structures. For more details on the Structural Approach, see Spencer Kagan's book, *Cooperative Learning.*

All the structures referred to in this book are described in detail with instructions for how to use them. Subsequent chapters that present activities for getting acquainted and developing vocabulary, grammar, and writing skills are based on the structures presented here.

The structures in this chapter are organized alphabetically for easy reference. As you use the activities described in the following chapters, you will probably want to turn back to the descriptions of the structures presented here. For these reasons, you will probably be referring to this chapter more than any other.

# 4-S Brainstorming

In 4-S Brainstorming every student on the team has a role to facilitate the creative potential of brainstorming. The students have gambits to say in the target language that encourage each other:

- **Speed**
"Let's hurry!"
- **Silly**
"Let's get crazy!"
- **Synergy**
"Let's build on that!"
- **Support**
"All ideas help!"

All ideas can be written down by one student who is the recorder, or each student can write down his or her own ideas using a small piece of paper for every idea. As soon as a student writes down one idea, s/he puts the paper in the middle of the team where later it can be categorized with similar ideas. Crazy ideas stimulate students to be creative and eliminate inhibitions.

### For more on
## 4-S Brainstorming

- Getting Acquainted  3: 2
- Writing Skills  6: 1

## *Sample Activities*
# 4-S Brainstorming:
### Ways to spend $1000

Students first brainstorm many ideas for spending $1000. Once the brainstorming is finished, they prioritize their five favorite suggestions and decide a corresponding dollar amount. Then have the teams decide exactly what they would buy with their $1000 and make a team drawing of the item(s). When making the drawing, each team member chooses a different color marking pen and uses only that color. Students are instructed that all four colors must appear in the final drawing about equally. Teams need to decide in advance what their picture will look like, and all team members participate in the drawing.

# 4-S Brainstorming:
### Who Are You?

Students brainstorm questions that they might ask someone they just met and really wanted to get to know. Have one team member volunteer to be the recorder. Give the class enough time for each team to generate at least eight questions. Encourage silly questions! Each team member selects two of the questions. Teams then pair up and interview each other.

# 4-S Brainstorming:
## Let's Vacation

Teams brainstorm places they would like to go for a team vacation. Once they have their lists, have the teams prioritize and select one vacation destination.

Next have teams 4-S Brainstorm activities they would do once they went there on holiday together. Teams can make a collage that illustrates their planned activities and their ideas about what it is like in their vacation spot.

# 4-S Brainstorming:
## Original Invention

Teams send a representative to the front of the class to blindly choose an item out of a shopping bag that the teacher holds. The bag contains some of the oddities from a

kitchen gadget drawer: melon baller, lemon wedge squeezer, garlic press, whisk, ice cream scoop, tea ball, or egg yolk strainer. Teams brainstorm unusual uses for the item using the 4-S Brainstorming structure.

Once a long list of unusual uses has been generated in every team, teams select their favorite use to create a T.V. advertisement to present to the class. The advertisement can include innovative packaging of the item, demonstrations for its use, a jingle that will help it sell, as well as a dynamic poster to motivate the consumer. This activity generates a lot of laughter as well as vocabulary expansion. Videos of the team presentations make interesting viewing for the class.

**NOTES:**

# Flashcard Game

To play the Flashcard Game all students first learn how to say exaggerated praises in the target language. "Is your name Einstein?" or "You sure are a genius!" Students are encouraged to create new praisers to surprise and delight teammates who in turn learn their vocabulary list all the faster for the encouragement and fun.

Create a class list of exaggerated praisers for a poster that can go on the classroom wall. Students refer to the poster for the Flashcard Game and other times as well. The list must be fairly long so that tutors will not repeat any praiser during a round of the Flashcard Game.

When you hear any student make up a new exaggerated praiser during the game, stop the class and recognize that student for her/his imagination. Have the student write the new praiser on the class poster. This positive attention will start all the students thinking of more creative ways to encourage each other, adding to their enthusiasm for learning vocabulary!

**For more on**
**Flashcard Game**

- Making Words Mine 4: 1
- Guided Grammar 5: 2
- Lesson Designs 7: 8

### Round 1: Maximum Cues
Students pair up and decide who will be the tutor first. The tutees give their cards to the tutors who hold up one card at a time, first showing the front of the card with the cue and then turning the card and saying the answer to the tutees. The tutors then turn the card around again, showing the front, and the tutees try to give the answer.

If the answer is correct, the tutor gives an exaggerated praise and the tutee earns the return of the flashcard. If the tutee does not give a correct response s/he is entitled to a "helper" rather than a "praiser". Helpers are hints of any kind including showing the back of the card again. If a helper is given, the card is not won back but placed at the bottom of the stack of flashcards to practice again.

When the tutee has won back all of his or her cards, the tutor and tutee switch roles.

### Round 2: Few Cues
After both students have played Round 1, they progress to Round 2. The game is played in the same way except that with fewer cues the students move from short to

long-termed memory. The tutors show the front of the card only, and the tutees try to remember the back. Exaggerated praisers or helpers follow every attempt.

## Sample Activities

# Flashcard Game:
## Vocabulary Review

The Flashcard Game is a fun way to memorize vocabulary. Having students break down the vocabulary list and make a flashcard for each word they don't know teaches many of the words right away. Have students play the Flashcard Game with every vocabulary list they need to learn.

# Flashcard Game:
## Irregular Verb Mastery

Have students play the Flashcard Game when they are learning difficult or irregular verb forms. They put the infinitive form on one side of the flashcard with the challenging subject pronoun written below it. On the answer side of the flashcard students write the subject pronoun first and the correct conjugation following it.

NOTES:

# Flashcard Game:
## Learning Foods

Using a magazine with many pictures of food, students make flashcards with a picture on one side and the vocabulary word on the other side. Allow them to select a few pictures of food vocabulary that are not identified in the text, but interest them individually. As they play the Flashcard Game, they will learn new words from each other's unique choices as well as review textbook vocabulary.

# Flashcard Game:
## Grammar Practice

The Color-Coded Co-op Card lesson design and the Flashcard Game with grammar content can help students when memorization is required. Students can make flash cards to study:

- Subject/verb agreement with regular and irregular verbs
- Verb ending transformation for various tenses.

# Guess-The-Fib

> I love strawberry shortcake.
> I love corn-on-the-cob.
> I love fried shrimp.

Guess-The-Fib is fun for students because they are searching for the meaning in each others sentences so that they can compare what is being said with what they know to be true about each other so that they can guess the fib. Each student prepares a list of three statements about themselves — two of the statements are true, and one of them is false. When making their list students try to select true statements that are unusual enough to possibly be mistaken for fibs, and make up a fib that is entirely believable.

Taking turns around the team, one student at a time reads their three statements as if they are all true. The other students on the team can talk to each other about which statement they think is the fib, but they do not have to have concensus. When they have decided which statement is not true they tell their guess to the author. If the author has fooled the teammates, the teammates applaud the author. If the teammates have guessed the fib, the author applauds them.

For more on
**Guess-The-Fib**
• Making Words Mine 4: 1

Writing the three statements can take a lot of time for some students, and for this reason is best done as part of a homework assignment or a sponge activity after finishing classwork. Any vocabulary theme offers a new opportunity for students to play Guess-The-Fib.

## Sample Activities
## Guess-The-Fib:
### Vocabulary Fun

**Furniture:** What's in (not in) my house (bedroom, living room, kitchen . . .)?

**Clothing and Colors:** What is he or she wearing (not wearing) today? And who am I talking about?
What's in (not in) my closet?

**Occupations:** What I would (would not) like to be when I grow up.

**Sports and Pastimes:** What I did (did not do) last summer.
What I would like (would not like) to do next summer.

**Around Town:** Where I am going (not going) this week.

**Food & Drink** Foods I love (hate) to eat.

**Family:** Relatives I am going to (not going to) visit this year.

# Inside-Outside Circle

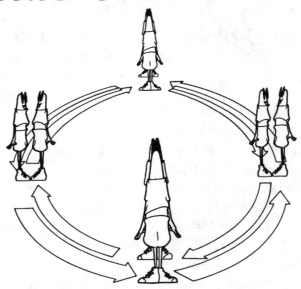

Half of the students in the class form a circle, shoulder to shoulder, facing outward. The other students each stand facing one person in the circle. The pairs briefly exchange greetings, interview each other, or review a few vocabulary or grammar items. At the teacher's signal the students stop talking. The teacher gives instructions for either the inside or outside circle to rotate to the left or right past a specific number of students before forming new pairs.

The repetition of vocabulary and grammatical structures in the target language with various other students provides a unique opportunity for students to rehearse and master new information.

## Sample Activities

### Inside-Outside Circle:

#### Introductions

Students take turns introducing themselves and greeting each other. Rotate each circle a few times

**For more on**
**Inside-Outside Circle**

• Getting to Know You 3: 1
• Making Words Mine 4: 2

to allow students to master the vocabulary as well as meet most of the class.

### Inside-Outside Circle:

#### Verb Practice

Each student writes an infinitive and subject pronoun on one side of a 3x5 card and the correct form of the verb on the other side. In their Inside-Outside Circles, students show the infinitive/pronoun side of their cards to their partners who give the correct verb form. The cards are then turned to show the answer correctly written. Have the students exchange cards with their partners before the circles rotate for subsequent rounds.

### Inside-Outside Circle:

#### Flashcard Game

Students choose their most difficult three or four flashcards to take to the Inside-Outside Circle. Unlike the Flashcard Game, in the Inside-Outside Circle, students quiz each other with the cards they have made instead of trading flashcards and winning them back.

## Team Inside-Outside Circle:

### Team Presentations

Teams each face one other team to present material as a group to another team. If presentations are normally 5 minutes, having each team come to the front of the class and share one at a time would take 40 minutes for eight teams, not counting transition times. In contrast, Team Inside-Outside Circle takes only 10 minutes for all teams to share. After the inside circle teams present, the outside circle teams present, and all teams have had a turn in a fourth the time!

NOTES:

## Inside-Outside Circle:

### Clothing Vocabulary

Students paste one of the following Clothing vocabulary pictures on one side of a 3 X 5 card and write the name of the item on the other side. In Inside-Outside circles, students quiz each other by first showing the picture side of the card. After their partner says or tries to guess the name of the article of clothing, the students turn the card around and show the correct spelling of the vocabulary word. Have students trade cards before rotating the circle each time. In this way the class can review a large vocabulary list and have a very good time doing it!

*Clothing*

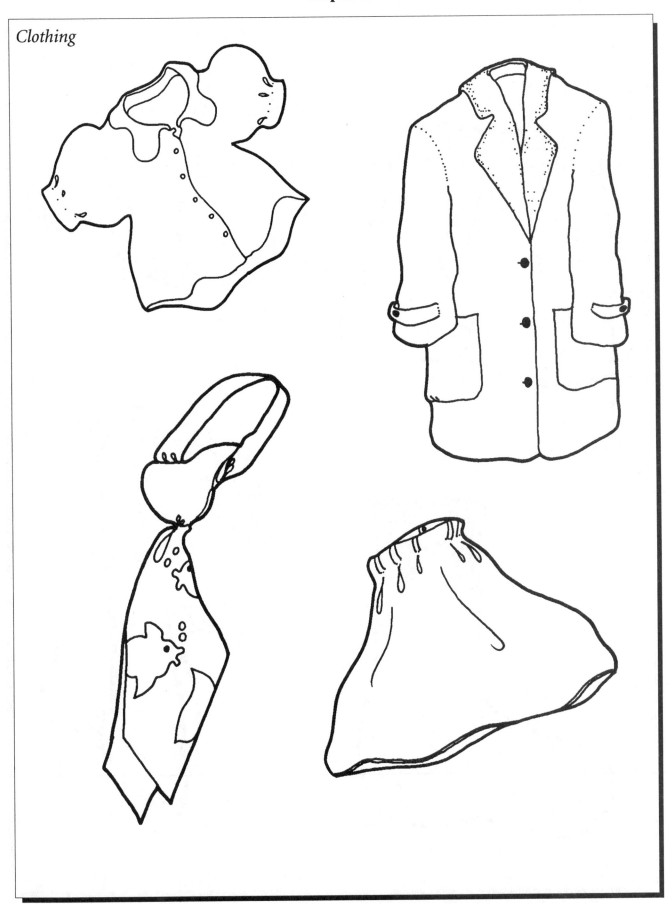

*Clothing*

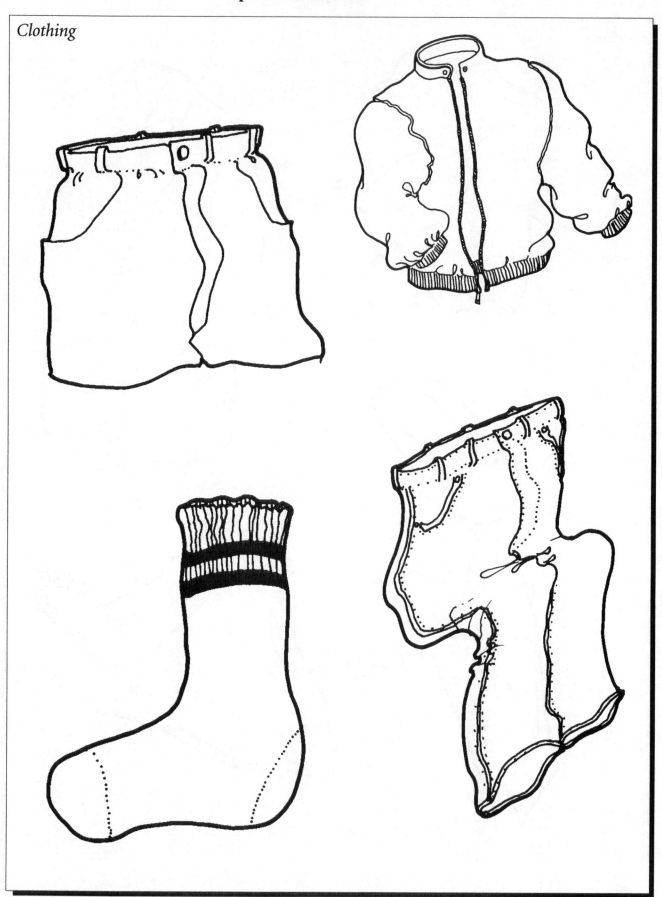

*Clothing*

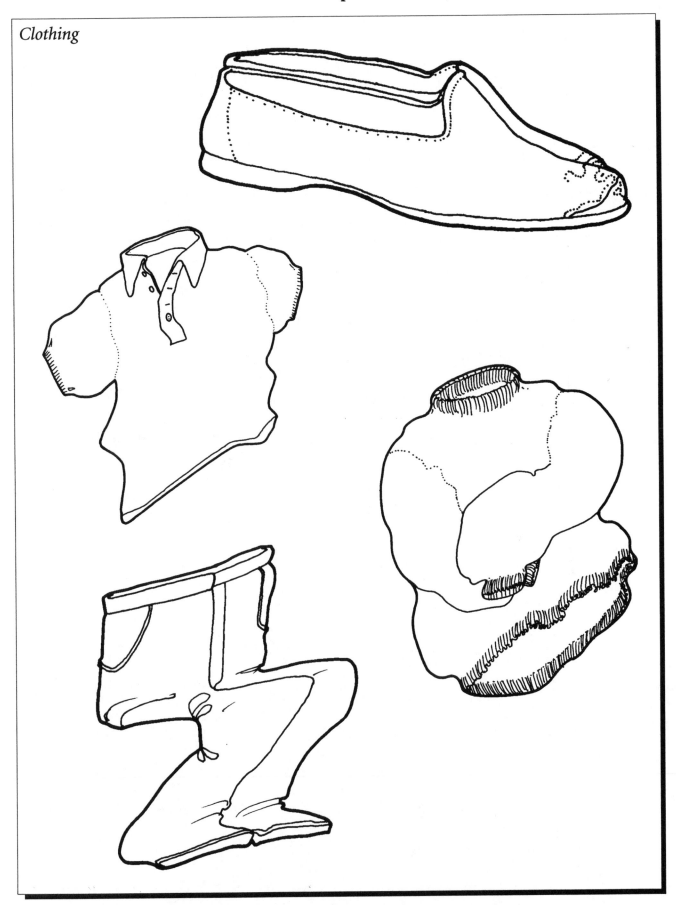

# Line-Ups

Line-Ups is an excellent classbuilding structure for practicing language. The mechanics of getting into a Line-Up involve a limited necessary vocabulary usually related to asking and answering only one simple question. The students know that they all belong in the Line-Up, but they must negotiate with each other to determine their exact position. When the class has been successful, there is only one line of students who are in place according to the announced criteria. The vocabulary necessary to request and share information to help each other get into the line can be easily identified, rehearsed in advanced, and put up on the overhead projector or chalkboard for students to refer to while getting into the line.

There is a wonderful self-esteem building aspect to lining up: the message is that each student in the room has a specific place that belongs to them. No Line-Up is complete until every student has taken their place. Reticent or shy students are drawn into the Line-Up by enthusiastic students who ask them the appropriate question and point out their spot in the line. After participating in many Line-Ups, each according to different criteria, students can draw the conclusions that they are all full members of a class in which they can have friendly interactions with anyone.

The first step in using this structure is for the teacher to announce how the class will be lining up. Once the entire class has lined up, starting at one end of the line have each student recite the information that determined their place in line. Intermediate and advanced students can interview each other in pairs or groups of four regarding some question that extends their sharing on the specified topic. For student accountability and to reinforce writing skills, after returning to their seats students can write down their position in the line, tell who was standing on either side of them, or what the person next to them said in answer to the interview question.

The following Line-Ups ideas are each followed by a suggested question that students will need to be able to ask and answer

## For more on
### Line-Ups

- Making Words Mine 4: 2
- Writing Skills 6: 1

as they line up. Interview questions for intermediate and advanced students to ask after lining up are also suggested.

## Alphabet

**1) Line up alphabetically by first, last, middle name:**
What is your first (last, middle) name?
*Intermediate:* Who is a famous person who shares your name?
*Advanced:* Why did your parents give you that name?

**2) Line up according to distance from school to where they were born:**
Where were you born?
*Intermediate:* What is the weather like there in Winter (Spring, Summer, Fall)?
*Advanced:* Why did your family move (not move) away from there?

**3) Line up according to distance from school to where they have travelled:**
How far have you travelled?
*Intermediate:* What is something interesting you saw when you travelled there?
*Advanced:* Would you go back there again? Why (why not)?

**4) Line up chronologically by birthdate:**
When is your birthday?
*Intermediate:* What is your favorite thing to do on your birthday?
*Advanced:* Tell me about the best thing that ever happened to you on your birthday.

## *Sample Activities:*
# *Line-Ups:*
### Poetry Line-Up
To practice a poem or rhyme that the students have already learned to read, cut up the poem into words or lines and give each student one. Students line up according to the order of the poem. When the line-up is complete have the class recite the poem together.

When the students have mastered lining up, select a poem that has only a few lines. Cut three or four copies of the poem into lines so that there will be several line-ups. There will be the additional challenge of students making sure that each line-up is a completed poem. Have the group of students with each particular line of the poem say that line together until the entire poem has been recited.

# *Line-Ups:*
### Sentence Building Line-Up
Students stand in team clusters around the room. Each team is given a group of cards with subject, verb, adjective, and noun cards taken from the vocabulary being studied by the class. The team members select cards that make a sentence. Each student hides their card until it is their team's turn to present their sentence. All together they students on a team turn their cards so that the other teams in the class can read their sentence. Put a rule in place that no team can repeat a sentence already presented by another. There may be some last minute scrambling!

 **NOTES:**

# Match Mine

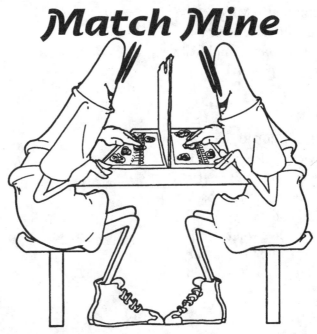

The Match Mine structure encourages accuracy of verbal communication. A barrier is set up between pairs of students so that they cannot see each other's paper. Students are given a grid and several shapes of familiar objects or pictures of target vocabulary. Students sit across from each other, screening their grids so that they can only see their own. One student is the sender and the other is the receiver. The sender arranges his or her shapes on the grid and then describes the pattern as clearly as possible so that the other students can recreate the design on the other side of the barrier. After they think they have finished, students remove the barrier and compare designs. Encourage students to analyze their process to discover how they could improve communication. To make the activity simpler, have one or more of the items already placed on the grid. For more challenge, increase the number of objects.

*Sample Activities*
# Match Mine:
## Clothing
Students each have a set of various items of clothing to place on a figure they hide behind their screens. Use pictures of models from a magazine as the figures and cut clothing items from other magazine photographs that will fit.

# Match Mine:
## My Town
For this Match Mine the grid is a simple street map with street names typical of a town where the target language is used. The shapes represent buildings and features of a town. One student places two buildings on the map and gives directions to the other student for how to get from one place to the other. Afterwards, both students compare maps and building placement.

*For more on*
## Match Mine
• Making Words Mine 4: 2

Another way to use this Match Mine activity is to have one student place several of the shapes on his or her map and simply tell the location for each. See page 4:3.

## *Match Mine:*

### Everyday Objects & People

Students select individual pictures of Everyday Objects & People vocabulary. Using a piece of notebook paper as a background, students send and receive Match Mine instructions. Students will be additionally practicing preposition vocabulary including above, next to, below, on the left, etc.

NOTES:

*Everyday Objects & People*

*Everyday Objects & People*

# Numbered Heads Together

1. Number off

2. Question Posed

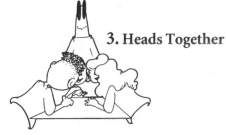

3. Heads Together

4. Number Called

Numbered Heads Together consists of four steps:
- Students number off.
- Teacher asks a question and gives a time limit.
- Students put their heads together and share the answer.
- Teacher calls a number to designate which student can answer for the team.

To share answers, teams simultaneously send the designated member to the chalkboard or butcher paper on the wall, and upon the teacher's signal, they write the appropriate word. All correctly spelled words earn points for their teams, and the student who first writes the word correctly can earn an additional point to motivate participation. Points earned in this way contribute towards a class goal to build class interdependence.

## *Sample Activities*
## Numbered Heads Together:
### What Time Is It?

When teaching students how to tell time in the new language, Numbered Heads Together helps them learn and reinforce their learning in a fun way.

Step 1: Using a blank clock face on the overhead or chalkboard, the teacher adds the hands to the clock.

Step 2: Students put their heads together and answer the question: What Time Is It?

Step 3: The teacher calls a number.

Step 4: The appropriate student from each team is responsible to report the group response.

---

*For more on*
## Numbered Heads

- Making Words Mine  4: 6
- Guided Grammar  5: 3

---

# Numbered Heads Together:

## Grammar Review

Simultaneous Numbered Heads is great for reviewing verb forms and grammatical structures before a test. To review verb forms the teacher gives the infinitive form of the verb first and then designates the subject. With their heads together students rehearse the answer.

Use Blackboard Share for simultaneity. Teams earn a recognition point for the correct answer as well as a bonus point for the team who put the correct answer up first.

# Numbered Heads Together:

## Verb Forms

Use Numbered Heads to help students practice conjugating regular and irregular verbs in any tense. The teacher writes the infinitive on the overhead or chalkboard and waits five seconds before adding a subject pronoun and tense.

# Numbered Heads Together:

## Vocabulary Review

Once students know what words are on the current vocabulary list, Numbered Heads is an excellent way for students to practice. The teacher shows an illustration or gives a definition for one of the words. After putting their heads together, teams simultaneously send the designated member to the chalkboard or butcher paper on the wall to write the appropriate word. All correctly spelled words earn points for the team, and the student who writes the word correctly first can earn an additional point to motivate participation.

# Numbered Heads Together:

## Sports & Pastimes

Make transparencies of the Sports & Pastimes vocabulary pictures. In Step 2 of Numbered Heads, put one of the pictures on the overhead projector. In Step 4 have the designated student from each team go to the chalkboard and write the name of the indicated sport of pastime.

*Variation:* Also indicate a subject pronouns and have the students write a complete sentence about doing the particular sport or pastime.

 NOTES:

*Sports & Pastimes*

*Sports & Pastimes*

*Sports & Pastimes*

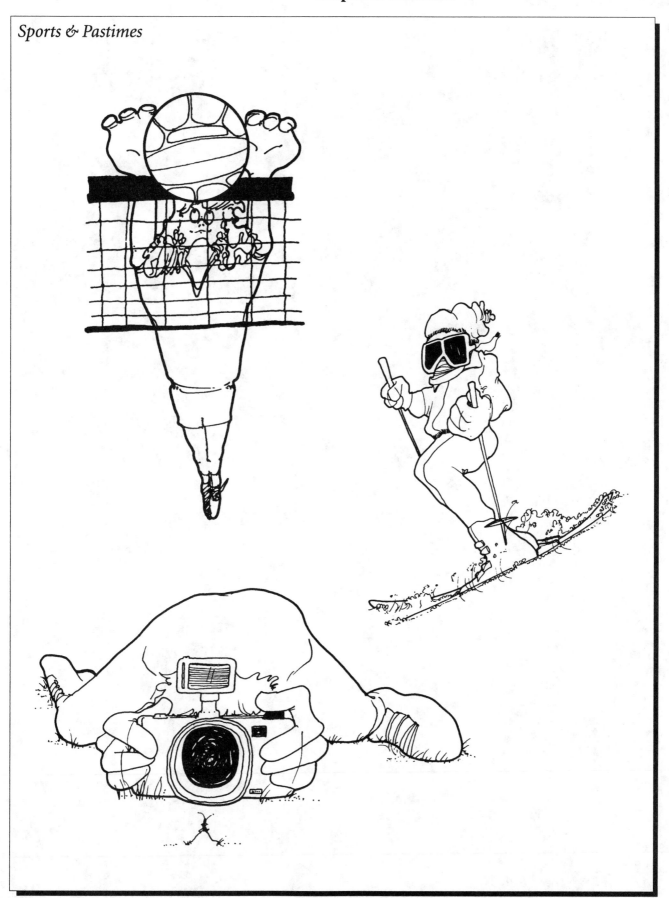

# Pairs Check

### 1. Individual Work

### 2. Coach Checks

### 3. Coach Praises

### 4. Individual Work

### 5. Coach Checks

### 6. Coach Praises

### 7. Pairs Check

### 8. Team Celebrates

Pairs Check is a good way to structure cooperative guided practice. Students work together in pairs to do practice exercises. One student acts as the coach as the other completes the first item. If the coach agrees with the answer, s/he gives a praiser. Then the two students switch roles, and work on the second item.

After two items are completed, the students wait for the other pair on their team to finish. The pairs check their answers and problem-solve any discrepancies. When they all agree, teams give a handshake, clap or short cheer to demonstrate to the class that they are moving on. Any misconceptions about the task are cleared up during the first practice items, and students can develop mastery through the remaining items.

teacher-made worksheet that will give students the opportunity to demonstrate understanding of a new grammatical structure. Model the guided practice activity for the class to make sure all students understand what is required. Pairs of students do the grammar exercise, checking with the other pair on the team after every two items.

## Pairs Check:
### Homework Check

Students can use the Pairs Check structure to discuss their homework efforts before the bell rings and during the first five minutes of class. If there are not four students with their completed assignment in a particular team, they can check their work in Step 7 with a pair from another team.

### Sample Activities
## Pairs Check:
### Guided Grammar Practice

Assign part or all of a grammar practice activity from the textbook or

NOTES:

# People Hunt

Students search for others who have certain characteristics indicated on a sheet with a space for a signature for each one. Include simple line drawings and cognates to cue beginning students. Possible characteristics can include: pets, time for getting up for school, number of brothers and sisters, and favorite radio station and television program. No student may sign any sheet more than once, and only the target language may be used.

People Hunt forms appropriate for beginning, intermediate and advanced foreign language students are included in Chapter 3. Translate the prompts into the target language and write them in the spaces provided. Use white-out or correction tape to cover the English versions. See People Hunt forms on pages 3:4, 3:5, and 3:6.

NOTES:

**For more on**

**People Hunt**

# Proactive Prioritizing

Proactive Prioritizing structures team discussions on selection of options for further group work. Referring to a list of possible choices, students make positive statements about the choices they prefer in a Roundrobin format. Rotate around the teams several times and require that each member advocate for at least two different choices to help them broaden their perspective.

## Sample Activities
### Proactive Prioritizing:
**Favorite Countries**

Looking at the completed world map with the countries highlighted where the target language is spoken, teams select the 5 countries they would most like to know more about. In a Roundrobin format students make positive statements of interest in particular countries such as: "I would like to know what the food is like in Guatemala," or "I want to know what the weather is like in Tibet." Rotate around the teams several times.

**For more on**
**Proactive Prioritizing**

• Lesson Designs 7: 5

# Q-Matrix

Chuck Wiederhold has authored a very ingenious way of accessing Bloom's Taxonomy and getting students to think critically about their classroom experiences. Chuck has designed a matrix of 36 question starters that incorporate six interrogative words with six different verbs in all the possible combinations. The Q-Matrix is available in English, Spanish, and French. The 36 combinations are presented in a variety of forms including Q-Chips, Q-Dice, Q-Spinners, Q-Quadrant Cards, and Q-Strips. Chuck Wiederhold has also written the book, *Cooperative Learning and Critical Thinking: The Question Matrix* which accompanies the Q-Materials Packet which provides a complete set for nine teams. Both are available from Kagan Cooperative Learning Company. You will be pleased to discover that students can often tell you more about what they think and have learned from writing original questions than answering teacher-made questions.

## *Sample Activities*
## Q-Matrix:
### Getting Acquainted

This activity gets students better acquainted and familiar with the range of Q-Matrix questions at the same time. One student stands in each team as the other members take turns asking questions to get to know them better. Have students put the Q-Chips face up in the middle of their teams. As the first student stands the other three each pick a Q-Chip of their choice and ask a question of their teammate. After hearing all the questions, the student being interviewed responds by answering only one of the questions. The Q-Chips that have been used are put aside, and the process is repeated with the other team members being interviewed one at a time.

## Q-Matrix:
### Literature Prediction

Using the Q-Dice students formulate questions about possible events of a story or book they will be reading in class. The activity has four rounds and every student writes four questions.

|  | EVENT | SITUATION | CHOICE | PERSON | REASON | MEANS |
|---|---|---|---|---|---|---|
| **PRESENT** | 1. What Is? | 2. Where/When Is? | 3. Which Is? | 4. Who Is? | 5. Why Is? | 6. How Is? |
| **PAST** | 7. What Did? | 8. Where/When Did? | 9. Which Did? | 10. Who Did? | 11. Why Did? | 12. How Did? |
| **POSSIBILITY** | 13. What Can? | 14. Where/When Can? | 15. Which Can? | 16. Who Can? | 17. Why Can? | 18. How Can? |
| **PROBABILITY** | 19. What Would? | 20. Where/When Would? | 21. Which Would? | 22. Who Would? | 23. Why Would? | 24. How Would? |
| **PREDICTION** | 25. What Will? | 26. Where/When Will? | 27. Which Will? | 28. Who Will? | 29. Why Will? | 30. How Will? |
| **IMAGINATION** | 31. What Might? | 32. Where/When Might? | 33. Which Might? | 34. Who Might? | 35. Why Might? | 36. How Might? |

## Q-Matrix

## Q-Matrix:
### Watching the Movie

Each team member gets a different Q-Quadrant card before starting to watch a movie in class. After significant parts of the film the teacher interrupts the movie and the students write a question starting with any Q-Matrix element on their Quadrant card. In teams students Roundrobin their questions before the teacher shows another section of the movie. Depending on the length of the movie, students will write three to five questions. Collect student questions at the end of the activity and ask some of them to the whole class to check comprehension or review the contents of the movie.

**Round 1:** The teacher reads the title of the book or story and students roll the Q-Dice and write a question about what they think the story will be about. Teams Roundrobin their questions.

**Round 2, 3, & 4:** The teacher reads two sentences of a descriptive paragraph about the story and students repeat the question writing and sharing process.

Use the Prediction Q-Strips instead of the Q-Dice to make the questions easier to write by limiting the potential combinations.

## The Q-Materials

# *Roundrobin*

#1 Shares

#2 Shares

#4 Shares

#3 Shares

Roundrobin is the oral counterpart of Roundtable. Students take turns around the team contributing answers or reading something they have written.

## *Roundrobin:*

### Verb Pass

To practice forms of irregular verbs, one student suggests a subject pronoun and the next teammate completes the conjugation with the correct form of the verb. That student then selects a different subject pronoun for the third teammate to complete. At first students may need to have the forms written on the chalkboard or on a piece of paper in the center of the team to prompt the correct responses. After some practice the prompt can be removed.

For a variation, instead of going in sequential order around the team, have students choose who will follow their lead. As a student says the subject pronoun of their choice, they

### For more on
## Roundrobin
- Getting to Know You 3: 1
- Making Words Mine 4: 2
- Lesson Designs 7: 6

can then actually pass a pen or pencil to another student to say the rest of the conjugation. In this way students cannot be sure when they will need to answer and will pay better attention to every turn.

## *Roundrobin:*

### Student Introductions

Introduce yourself on the first day of class using only the target language. Have a few of the students demonstrate comprehension by volunteering to introduce themselves. Choose the team that had the volunteer who performed with the most confidence to model Roundrobin for the class. Each student introduces her/himself going around the team. Have teams pair and repeat the Roundrobin student introductions.

## *Roundrobin:*

### Days of the Week, Months of the Year, Ordinal Numbers, Cardinal Numbers

Teams recite the designated list of words in a roundrobin fashion. Different students begin additional rounds so that everyone ends up needing to know all the names of the days. Variations include:

1. Start the list at a different point.
2. Recite the list backwards.
3. Use a race format — teams recite the list three times in a row and raise their hand when they've finished.

**NOTES:**

# Roundtable

#1 Contributes

#2 Contributes

#4 Contributes

#3 Contributes

## Step 1: The Problem

The teacher asks a question with many possible answers, such as name all the sports you can, or list any items you can identify in the classroom.

## Step 2: Students Contribute

Teams have one piece of paper and one pen or pencil that rotate around the team. Each student writes one answer on the list and passes the pen and paper. If any student is having difficulty thinking of what to write, the teammates can make suggestions.

Teams can receive recognition for various characteristics of their lists. Recognize speed, improvement in speed, and spelling accuracy to generate the excitement of working together. Recognize teams with the longest word, the shortest word, the most uncommon word or any other unusual aspect to stimulate creativity.

### *Sample Activities*
## *Roundtable:*
### Alphabetical Parts of Speech

Parts of speech lend themselves to the pace of the Roundtable format. Teams Roundtable nouns, verbs or adverbs beginning with each letter of the alphabet. For a variation, reverse the order of the alphabet or start with a different letter than "A".

## *Simultaneous Roundtable:*
### Who is the Teacher?

Each team will simultaneously create Roundtable descriptions of four different teachers following a model. Every student has a sheet of paper where they will write one sentence to start a descriptive paragraph about a special teacher. After each sentence is written the papers are passed to the next student on the team until every

*For more on*
## Roundtable
- Guided Grammar 5: 2

student has contributed one sentence to each paragraph. Students can consult with each other regarding unfamiliar teachers.

**Round 1:** The name of one of their teachers at school and their classroom number.

**Round 2:** The subject s/he teaches.

**Round 3:** A physical characteristic.

**Round 4:** Descriptive sentence about the course s/he teaches.

After Round 4, students take turns reading their descriptions to each other on the team. Then have teams pair and read their descriptions again.

# Simultaneous Roundtable:
## Cinquain Poems

A cinquain poem contains five lines written according to a model. In this activity each team will write four poems simultaneously, with every team member contributing at least one line to each. After each line is written the papers are passed to the next student on the team until the poems are finished. Poems are written in a diamond design and can be displayed as posters to decorate the classroom.

**Round 1:** One noun - the subject and title of the poem.

**Round 2:** Two adjectives describing the noun.

**Round 3:** Three present participles describing the noun.

**Round 4:** One four word sentence about the subject.

**Round 5:** One adjective - another way of expressing the title of the poem.

> *Birthday*
> *fun, happy*
> *eating, playing, singing*
> *My own special day.*
> *Great!*

# Simultaneous Roundtable:
## Group Grid

For team identity building, each team makes a large grid on a piece of butcher paper that will chart information about the members. Teams draw a grid with one horizontal column for every team member and ten vertical columns. Students enter their names in the far left spaces and write their personal data in the columns to the right. The teams can decide what information to collect from a list of choices that can include:

- Age
- Number of brothers and sisters
- Name of the street they live on
- The name of the city they were born in
- Favorite food
- Least favorite food
- Favorite T.V. show
- Favorite music group
- Favorite color
- Favorite subject in school
- Kind of pet
- Favorite spectator sport
- Favorite pastime
- Favorite farm/zoo animal
- Height
- Favorite amusement park attraction

*Variation:*

# Rallytable:
## Occupations Word Guess

Referring to the vocabulary pictures for Occupations, students Rallytable a list of yes/no questions that they will ask of the other pair of students on their team to be able to guess which occupation is pictured inside an envelope. First one student writes a question, then passes the paper to their partner who will say and write another question. When both pairs have prepared a list of at least six questions, they are ready to receive an envelope with a picture of one of the occupations inside. Both pairs of students check to see which picture is included in their envelope, and then they take turns asking their questions until each pair guesses the occupation correctly.

**NOTES:**

*Occupations*

Occupations

*Occupations*

# Roundtable/Roundrobin

Saturday!

Combine the Teambuilding structures of Roundtable and Roundrobin to make an excellent and often-used Mastery Structure. Since Roundtable requires a quick pace to maintain student interest, it is best used as a review activity. As students write the appropriate word, they also need to pronounce it. This makes the activity Roundrobin at the same time. Recognize speed, improvement in speed, and spelling accuracy to generate excitement working together. Once students are familiar with Roundtable/Round-robin, use it as a sponge activity to soak up extra time before the end of class, or as an initial class activity to get the students thinking in the target language.

that will clarify and demonstrate their understanding of the content. Using a Roundtable/Roundrobin structure, teams write their own version of:

- What might happen to the main character in 5 years.
- The dialogue at a particularly important part of the story.
- An alternate ending.

Team presentations can imitate or parody what they saw in the film.

## Roundtable/ Roundrobin:
### Alphabet Categories

Challenge students to generate an A to Z list of 26 words associated with a specific activity identified by the teacher. Christmas, Summer Vacation, and Birthdays are examples of titles of categories that will generate a variety of responses. Encourage students to help each other with all the letters. Reward teams for finishing first, their longest word, most creative word, and their most difficult word to formulate.

**For more on**
## Roundtable/Roundrobin

- Getting to Know You 3: 2
- Making Words Mine 4: 5
- Guided Grammar 5: 2
- Writing Skills 6: 2
- Lesson Designs 7: 3

## Sample Activities
## Roundtable/ Roundrobin:
### After the Movie

After students see a film in the target language they can work in teams to create presentations

# Roundtable/ Roundrobin:

## Days and Months

After teaching the days of the week and the months of the year have students Roundtable/Roundrobin the lists. For each round have the student start the list with a different day or month in the sequence. The students can write the lists forward or backward to vary the challenge.

# Roundtable/ Roundrobin:

## Dialogue

Show pictures of interesting-looking natives from a country where the target language is spoken and explain that they are going to have a conversation. Teams create a dialogue using a Roundtable/ Roundrobin format by first answering the questions: Who?, What?, When?, Where?, and Why? They proceed to write a script of a minimum number of verbal exchanges between the characters. There should be one character for each member of the team. Current topics of study in vocabulary and grammatical structures can be designated by the teacher to be included in the dialogue. Teams can present their dialogues using costumes and/or props.

# Roundtable/ Roundrobin:

## Grammar Practice

When learning the conjugations of verbs Roundtable/Roundrobin is an especially good way to check for understanding. The teacher presents direct instruction with particular verbs and then gives an unfamiliar example for students to Roundtable/ Roundrobin. By circulating around the room while the teams help each other with the forms, the teacher can assess comprehension and address individual questions while the entire class is actively involved with guided practice.

Roundtable/Roundrobin with verb conjugations is also a good way to begin class as a brief, involving activity that helps students transition into thinking in the target language.

# Roundtable/ Roundrobin:

## Happy Endings

Students read a short story appropriate to their ability level from which the ending has been omitted. Teams Roundtable/ Roundrobin the final paragraph(s) and present their ending to the class. Encourage use of props, humor and dramatic flair. Since every team has the same story to start with, they will be familiar with the context and vocabulary applied to the variety of endings.

# Roundtable/ Roundrobin:

## In a Hurry! (Reflexive Verbs)

Students imagine that they have been at the beach all day and only have a few minutes to get ready to go to a party. They Roundtable/Roundrobin all the necessary activities that must be completed before they are ready.

# Roundtable/ Roundrobin:

## Need to Know

Students imagine that they have been hired to direct the Office of Tourism for the country they have selected. Teams Roundtable/Roundrobin all the aspects of a country that they would need to learn about. The list could include food, natural wonders, cities, tourist sights, sports, native costumes, music, dances, art, literature, famous people, and government.

Each student selects the one area of most interest to him or her. Only one student may work on any particular aspect. They need to know that they will be responsible for creating some type of demonstration to illustrate the area they choose.

# Roundtable/ Roundrobin:
## Post-Christmas Review
After Christmas vacation students enjoy Roundtable/Roundrobin as a way to get back into the practice of thinking in the target language. Teams can Roundtable/Roundrobin every word they can think of that begins with a certain letter. Start with easy letters like S, T and R, and proceed with more unusual letters like C, G and L. Recognize teams who have the longest lists, the most unusual words, the longest words and the shortest words.

# Simultaneous Roundtable/ Roundrobin:
## Stop Story
Give every team a copy of an interesting picture. In Simultaneous Roundtable fashion every student on the team starts to write their own story about the picture. After three minutes the teacher calls "stop," and students take their pen off the paper at whatever point they are in the sentence. The stories are rotated to the next team member who has a chance to read what has been started and then has three more minutes to add another part. After every student has contributed at least once to every story, the teams Roundrobin all four sto-

ries. The best of the four can be selected and presented to the class in a simple reading, or as a skit with props and costumes.

# Roundtable/ Roundrobin:
## Uncommon Commonalities
Give every team a sheet of blank paper. Have them fold the paper in fourths and draw a rectangle in the middle. Students take turns around the group listing facts about themselves that they write or make a line drawing of on the fourth of the paper closest to them outside of the rectangle. Teams continue until they discover one unusual fact that all team members share. This fact is then written in the center rectangle as well as in each member's quadrant. Teams can continue the process to see how many uncommon commonalities they share.

# Roundtable/ Roundrobin:
## What's Going On?
Each team receives a fairly detailed picture with many activities depicted. Teams Roundtable/Roundrobin a list of all nouns, verbs, and/or adjectives illustrated. More advanced students can then Roundtable/ Roundrobin a story about the picture using their previous lists to begin sentences.

# Roundtable/ Roundrobin:
## What's in Store?
Teams Roundtable/Roundrobin everything they might see if they went into a particular kind of store at a mall. Teams then identify any categories that link items on the list. Students can choose minitopics from these categories. Responsibility for minitopic

presentation can include providing the props, costumes and advertising posters that will distinguish their store. Students can script possible interactions with customers so they are prepared to respond.

# Roundtable/ Roundrobin:
## Where in the World?

Locate a one-page world map, highlight the countries where the target language is spoken. Many foreign language textbooks have a map like this at the beginning of the book. Copy the map without names of the countries so that students can try to think of them.

Teams Roundtable/Roundrobin the map helping each other put as many of the countries' names as they can think of together. When all teams have as many as they can think of, show a regular world map so they can fill in the rest of the names.

# Roundtable/ Roundrobin:
## Who's Who?

Each team receives a different picture portraying a variety of vocabulary they are

NOTES:

familiar with. Department store catalogs are a good source. Teams Roundtable/ Roundrobin descriptions of the picture they have including the illustrated clothing, the setting, any activities they recognize, or labels for any of the people pictured. After the descriptions are finished the teacher collects the pictures and mixes them with a few that were not given to any team. All the pictures are placed in front of the class. Teams divide their Roundtable/ Roundrobin list so that each member reads part of the description. After each team reads their list the other teams put their heads together to decide which picture has been described. Pictures can be more or less similar to vary difficulty.

# Roundtable/ Roundrobin:
## Word Guess

Place a picture of one of the words from the students' vocabulary list in an envelope. Teams Roundtable/Roundrobin questions they could ask to identify the item. Teams ask one question each until the word is guessed.

# Same-Different

Two pictures are created that are basically the same with a variety of specific differences that when discovered will elicit use of target vocabulary and grammatical structures. One copy of each picture is provided to each pair of students on a team of four. The pairs sit opposite each other with a barrier between them so that they cannot see the other pair's paper. The more differences, the easier it will be for students to participate.

Students take turns making statements about their picture that the other team members confirm or amend to discover the differences.

## *Sample Activities*
## Same-Different:
### Family
After teaching the vocabulary associated with the names of members of the family,

have students do the Same-Different activity on the following pages. They will be practicing the identified words while they enjoy comparing their pictures.

## Same-Different:
### Holiday Words
The two pictures located on pages 1:46 and 1:47 come from Spencer Kagan's book, *Same-Different, Holidays Edition: A Communication Building Structure*, available through **Kagan Cooperative Learning**. This is an excellent source of a variety of Same-Different pictures that give students many differences to discuss.

NOTES:

## Same-Different

*Same-Different: Family Picture 1*

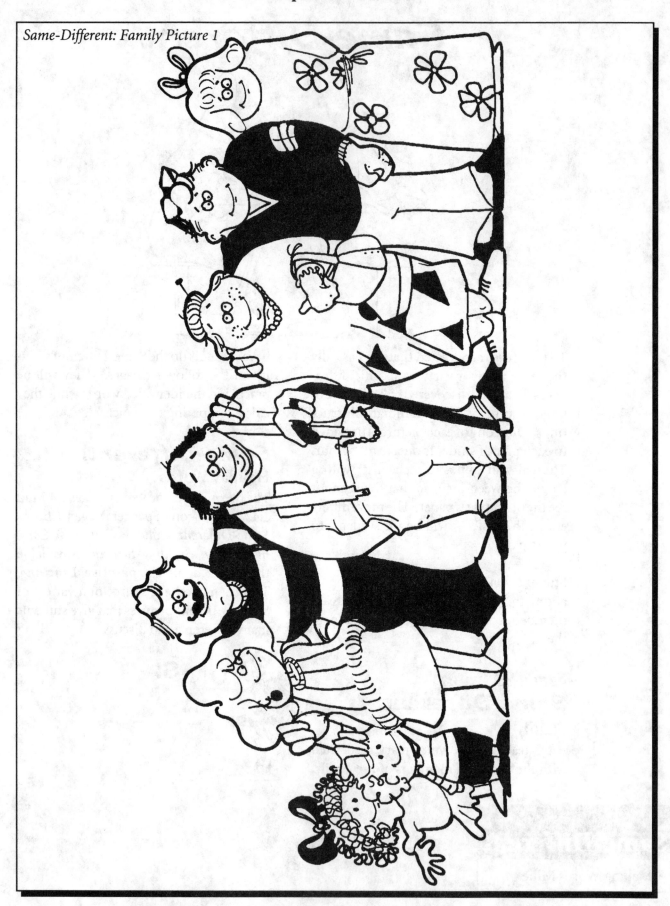

*Same-Different: Family Picture 2*

*Same-Different Picture 1*

# Christmas

*Same-Different Picture 2*

# Christmas

# Christmas

## Same

1. _____
2. _____
3. _____
4. _____
5. _____
6. _____
7. _____
8. _____
9. _____
10. _____
11. _____
12. _____
13. _____
14. _____
15. _____
16. _____
17. _____
18. _____
19. _____
20. _____

## Different

1. _____
2. _____
3. _____
4. _____
5. _____
6. _____
7. _____
8. _____
9. _____
10. _____
11. _____
12. _____
13. _____
14. _____
15. _____
16. _____
17. _____
18. _____
19. _____
20. _____

# Send-A-Problem

Send-A-Problem is a structure through which students demonstrate understanding of new structures by creating examples of their own. They practice enthusiastically when the exercises have been written by their classmates. When it is time in the lesson for guided practice activities, teams write their own exercises using the textbook activities as models. Using a Simultaneous Roundtable/Roundrobin format, teams generate four different exercises with one rotation. At first it may be necessary for teams to first do some of the textbook examples so they can apply the model. The teacher is very active during Send-A-Problem to ensure that team-generated exercises are correct and follow the model. After each team member has written four to six items, the sheets are collected and the bottom part containing the answers is torn away. The top part with the guided practice items is then passed to another team. If a team has difficulty, they can consult with the team who sent the problem.

**For more on**
## Send-A-Problem

• Making Words Mine 4: 6
• Guided Grammar 5: 3

## Sample Activities
## Send-A-Problem:
### Getting Around Town

This activity helps students master the vocabulary associated with giving directions and the features of a town. Every team member has a town map marked with common locations associated with a town, including the library, school, supermarket, restaurant, bank, hotel, etc. Each team member selects any location and writes the directions from that place on the map to any other destination. When they have finished, the four descriptions are sent to the next team. The team members then read the directions given them and decide which two locations were selected. On a blank copy of the map each student can draw the route suggested in their problem. Students can be very creative with how to get from one spot to another!

## Send-A-Problem:
### Grammar Practice

At the point in the grammar lesson where the class needs guided practice, assign a few key items from a textbook or teacher-made worksheet. You may want to use Pairs Check to formalize students helping each other with the exercise. When the students have demonstrated that they can do the provided exercise with confidence, have them create their own sample exercises following the model given using Send-A-Problem. Be sure to monitor student participation to check correctness and assist with clarification.

## Send-A-Problem:

### Food & Drink

Give each team four of the following Food & Drink vocabulary pictures. Teams si-multaneously Roundtable four lists of sentences that describe the item with out saying what it is. Each student writes one sentence for a particular picture and then pass it to the next student until each item has four description sentences. Teams collect and pass in the pictures and share each description with a different other team. Each team should receive four paragraphs. Each team member reads the description out loud and tries to guess what the food or drink item is. The sending team can verify the answer if there is a question.

NOTES:

*Food & Drink*

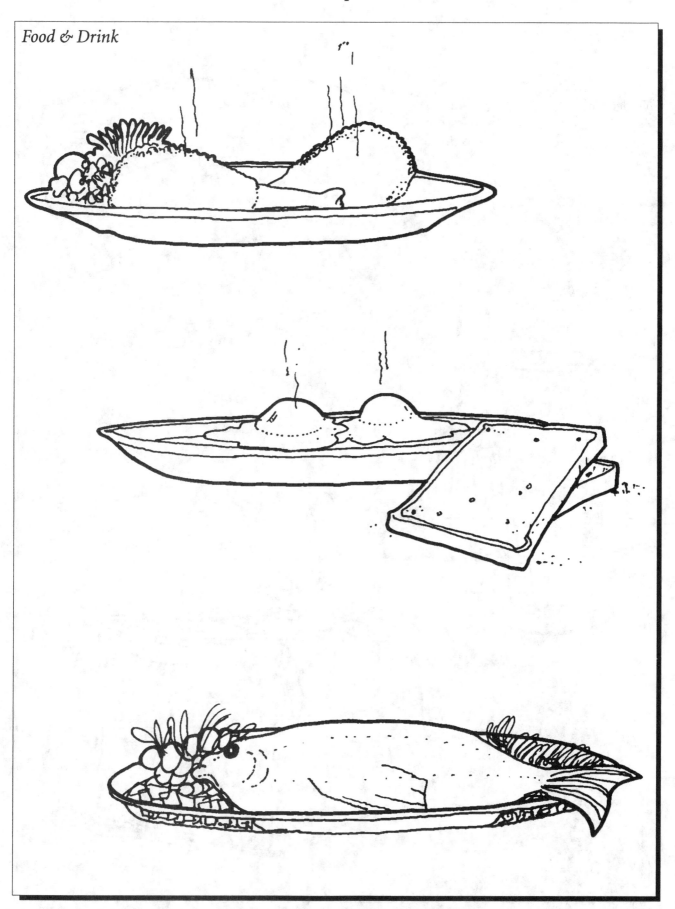

*Food & Drink*

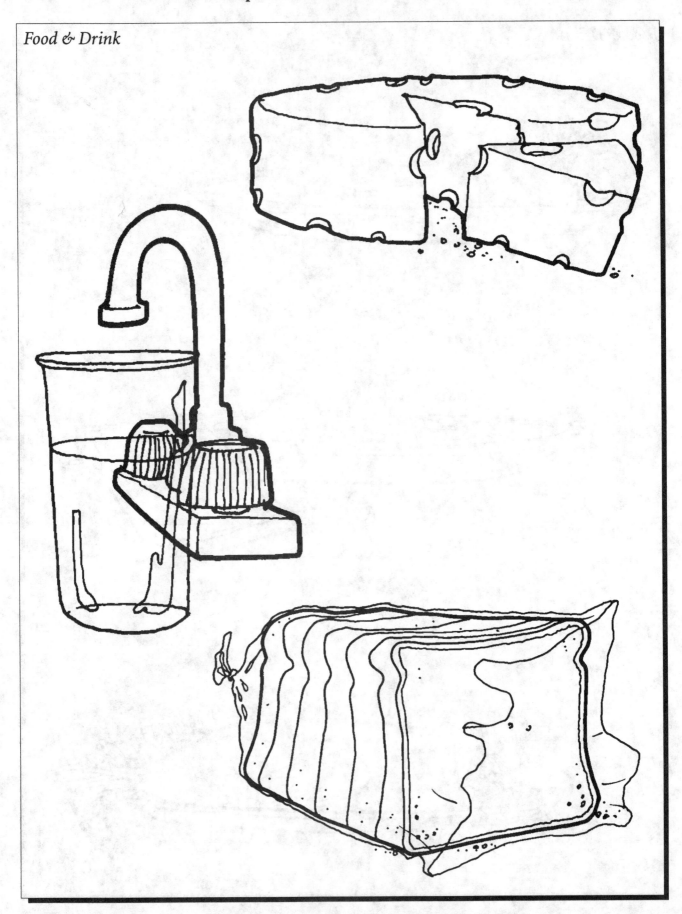

*Food & Drink*

**Julie High:** *Second Language Learning through Cooperative Learning*©
Publisher: Kagan Cooperative Learning • 1 (800) WEE CO-OP

# Simultaneous Sharing

When teams work together cooperatively, they generate ideas and create projects that need to be shared with the class. But when the entire class listens to one team present, much class time is used and students tend to lose interest. There are various forms of Simultaneous Sharing that can be used to provide every team the same opportunity to share with the class at the same time.

## Variations
### Blackboard Share

This form of Simultaneous Sharing is used especially with Numbered Heads Together, and can just as easily be used after Team Discussion.

In Blackboard Share each team sends one representative to the board or chart paper placed around the room and simultaneously posts their responses.

*Sample Activities*
### Blackboard Share
**Simultaneous Numbered Heads- What Time Is It?**

Step 1: Using a blank clock face on the overhead or chalkboard, the teacher adds the hands to the clock.

Step 2: Students put their heads together and answer the question: What Time Is It?

Step 3: The teacher calls a number.

Step 4: The appropriate student from each team goes to the chalkboard or chart paper to a team spot to write their answer.

### Gallery Tour

In this form of Simultaneous Sharing students move about the room in their teams to see the products of other teams. The team products can be displayed at their desks with a response sheet available for feedback from touring teams.

*For more on*
**Simultaneous Sharing**

• Lesson Designs 7: 4, 6

# Gallery Tour:

## 'Round the World

Divide the class by asking for half the teams to volunteer to do their presentations. On a designated day the first half of the teams will present while the other half tours the exhibitions. The touring students have the questions prepared by each presenting team to answer when they visit their presentation.

When students come dressed in costume, provide ethnic foods, play regional music and speak in the target language it will seem like the class is a foreign bazaar. Either the next day or the next week have the teams switch roles. Be sure to invite parents, the principal, other teachers, school board members, and local politicians if the class is willing.

# Roam the Room

When teams have created a display of some type, at the teacher's signal the students move around the room to see what other teams have made. If there are questions to be asked of the teams, half of the team's members can roam while the other pair stays with the project. At the teacher's signal the pairs switch roles. The teams can provide the teacher with questions that other students should be able to answer after seeing their project. With a worksheet of these questions in hand, students will be sure to observe each other's projects carefully. When everyone in the room has seen all other teams' projects, students return to their teams and share their observations.

# Roam the Room:

## Take A Look

Perhaps at the beginning of the following class period, students move around the room as individuals to view posters made by other teams. After a few minutes teams assemble and Roundtable/Roundrobin to share positive statements about what they have seen. The most positive statement about each poster is written on a separate piece of paper. When all teams have finished, the compliments are delivered to the other teams.

# Two Stay, Two Stray

In this variation of Gallery Tour, half the team members tour while the other stays with their team display to interact with the visiting members from other teams. On the same or a different day the team members switch roles so that everyone gets to tour the room and present the team product as well.

# Two Stay, Two Stray:

## Shopping Day in a Mall Simulation

During the simulation, two members of the team stay with the store to deal with the customers. Every team needs to prepare facsimiles of foreign currency in advance so that each member will have money to go shopping, and every store will have money to make change. Items for sale have a 3x5 card in front of them with the name of the item on it. No prices are advertised so that shoppers must ask for the price of the item. Every student must buy at least one thing from three stores.

Each student writes on a piece of paper what they bought, the price and the reason they bought it. Students do not remove purchases from the store. Shop owners keep track of what items have sold. When half the class period is over, shoppers and shop owners switch roles and the process is repeated.

 **NOTES:**

# Spend-A-Buck

When teams need to select one choice from several possibilities, Spend-A-Buck is a good way for students to come to consensus without debate. Students each take four small pieces of paper and put their initials on one side. Each student may spend up to three of their "quarters" to vote for any one choice. The choice with the most votes becomes the team choice. Teams may need to play a second or third round of Spend-A-Buck if the first round doesn't determine a clear favorite. In that case, the choices with the fewest votes are eliminated, and the students choose from only the few most popular selections.

## *Sample Activities*
## Spend-A-Buck
### Choose A Store

In the At the Mall Co-op Co-op Lesson Design (Chapter 7) students use Spend-A-Buck to select the particular store that they will simulate for a class tour. After teams have Roundtabled a list of all the kinds of stores they

have ever seen at a mall, they use the Spend-A-Buck structure to select their team's favorite.

## Spend-A-Buck
### Country Selection

Have the teams use Spend-A-Buck to determine which country they would like to study in depth together. When a team has selected its country, they put their team name and the name of the country on a large piece of butcher paper or chart paper. Only one team can sign up to research any particular country, so the first team to make a particular choice has priority.

NOTES:

**For more on**
## Spend-A-Buck

• Lesson Designs 7: 3

# Story Scramble

Select a story appropriate to the proficiency level of the students. Cut up a copy for each team into 4 strips. Mix up the strips and place them in an envelope. Team members each take one strip out of the envelope at a time and read it to the team. The teams then decide the sequence of the parts in the story. To increase the difficulty of the activity, select a longer story and cut the story into 8 or 12 strips, or choose a story in which the order of events could vary without changing the outcome. Each team member can read his or her part of the story as a team presentation.

## _Sample Activities_
## Story Scramble:
### Poetry
Find poems in the target language that have four to twelve lines to cut up into strips. Let teams suggest alternate ways to structure the poem.

## Story Scramble:
### Cultural Selection
Foreign language and ESL textbooks usually include brief sections that address interesting cultural differences in countries where the target language is spoken. Make a copy of one of the articles for each team and use Story Scramble. After the teams have discussed the correct order of the article, focus their attention on the original source so they can see the article printed in its entirety.

NOTES:

**For more on**
**Story Scramble**
• Writing Skills 6: 3

# Team Projects

There are a variety of team projects which facilitate language acquisition. Two of my favorites are Team Collage and Team Draw.

## 1. Team Collage

When a team presentation could include an art project, students bring magazine pictures, photographs and other items to create a collage together. On the specified day, teams Roundrobin the articles they have gathered and share why they brought those particular items to contribute to the poster. Teams discuss a plan for the poster before they begin pasting. Display the posters as soon as they are created. Encourage teams to add to their poster in the ensuing days since the synergy of the experience may prompt them to think of more possibilities.

### Sample Activities

## Team Collage:
### Our Team

A great activity for team identity building! Using newspapers and maga-zines in the target language and construction paper, students find and cut out letters that spell their team name. Each team member also cuts out two words that describe themselves as well as two pictures showing activities they like to do and two more pictures showing activities they would like to do in the future. Teams Roundtable a paragraph describing their collage with each student contributing at least two sentences.

## Team Collage:
### Our Country

Students gather information on a country where the target language is spoken from travel books, encyclopedias, foreign consulates, magazines, interviews with people who have lived in their chosen country, and interviews with teachers. Each student brings a selection of materials to class to create a team poster about the country. Encourage students to bring various pictures and small items other than pictures to mount on their posters. The poster can show the four distinct areas of study in the corners. As the pictures show elements that connect more than one area, they can

**For more on**
## Team Projects
• Making Words Mine 4: 7
• Lesson Designs 7: 5

be placed more towards the center of the poster.

## Team Collage:

### Home Improvement

Teams can use the following vocabulary pictures to decorate rooms of a house. Each team receives a large sheet of paper and a different color of marker pen for every team member. Each team member can only use the marker they select as they draw together an outline of a house with rooms that they can decorate with the vocabulary pictures. Each team member selects three of the following pictures that they will place on the house collage. If the students want to decorate the pictures, they will need to cooperate in asking each other to apply each of the available marker colors. Once they have place the pictures, teams Roundtable a description of their house. Each team member contributes one sentence at a time until there are at least three sentences per student included in the description. Teams stand to show their collage and each student reads an equal number of sentences in the description. Have the teams post their houses on the classroom wall until the next vocabulary unit.

## 2. Team Draw

After vocabulary on a certain theme has been presented teams can create a picture together that they will present orally to the class. Each team member chooses a different color pen, and any one color can only be put in the picture by the team member who has that pen. As teams present their drawing to the class, each member contributes one or more sentences to the description.

_Sample Activities_

## Team Draw:

### Team Dream Home

After vocabulary associated with the house is presented, teams create a dream home with rooms, furniture and architecture that all members agree would be a special place to live.

## Team Draw:

### Simultaneous Team Draw: Imaginary Friend

With this activity students can practice vocabulary associated with describing appearance. Teams simultaneously make four drawings and write accompanying descriptions with every team member contributing one-fourth of each. Each student has one piece of blank paper to start, and after each round the papers are passed to the next team member.

**Round 1:** The students draw a face and write a sentence giving the person's name and describing his or her personality using current vocabulary.

**Round 2:** The papers are passed to the next person on each team who adds hair to the drawing and writes a sentence saying what color hair the person has.

**Round 3:** The next team members add a body with shirt and pants or skirt and describe the person's size.

**Round 4:** The fourth person to add to the drawing identifies the sport the person likes to play and adds a drawing of a corresponding piece of sporting equipment.

Students read the descriptions of the completed drawings to each other in their teams and post the drawing on the wall.

 NOTES:

*House*

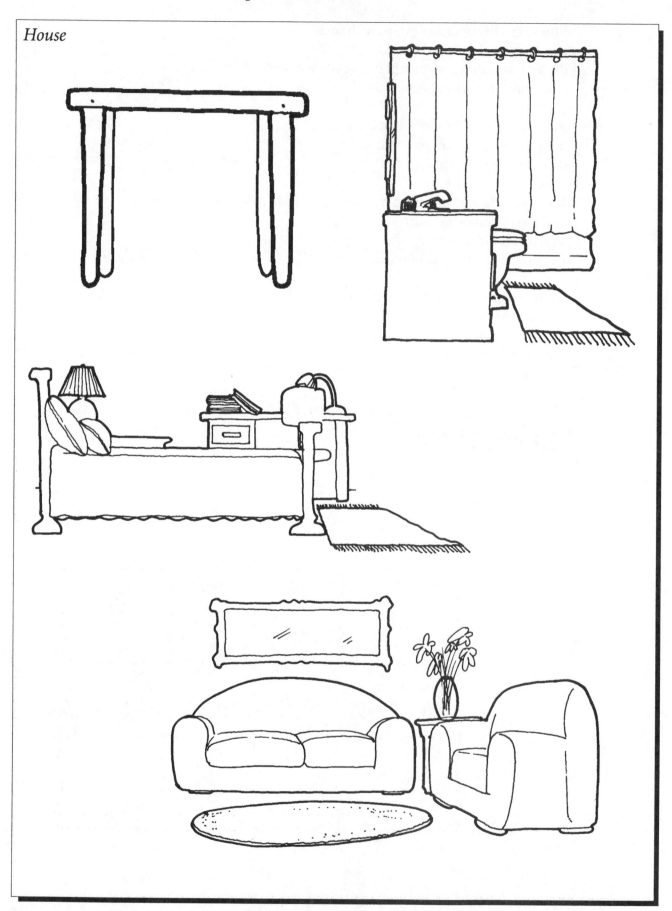

*House*

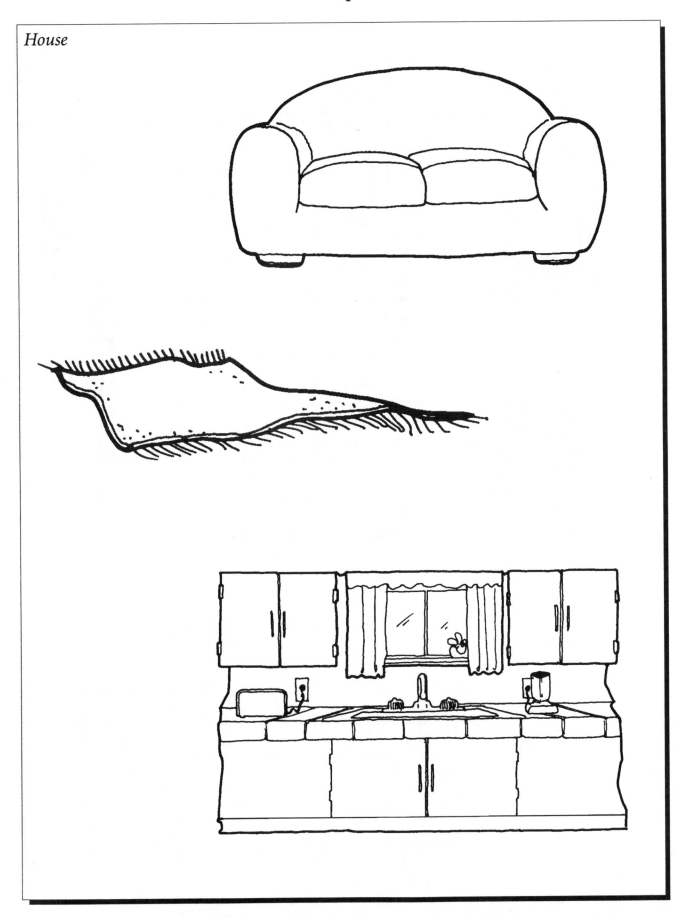

*House*

# Three-Step Interview

### Step 1:  One Way Interview

### Step 2:  The Reverse

### Step 3:  Roundrobin

#1 Shares

#2 Shares

#3 Shares

#4 Shares

## Step 1:  One Way Interview
Students are in pairs, one is the interviewer, the other is the interviewee.  The interviewer takes notes of the responses to use for paraphrasing later to the whole team.

## Step 2:  The Reverse
Students reverse roles.

## Step 3:  Roundrobin
Students paraphrase what they learned about their teammate to their team.

### *Sample Activities*
## Three-Step Interview:
### Getting To Know You
Have every team member select four questions from the brainstorming list and write them on a separate piece of paper with room for answers.  Students pair up and interview each other using their chosen questions.  They make

notes of the answers to help them paraphrase to the whole team.

## Three-Step Interview
### Famous Person
After doing the Who Am I? Famous Natives activity, have students interview each other, answering questions as if they were the famous person whose name was pinned on their back.

## Three-Step Interview:
### New Grammar Practice
As students learn new tenses Three-Step Interview is an excellent way to give them practice with the new verb structures.  Teams first Roundtable/Roundrobin questions they would like to ask each other within the new time reference: present, past, future, conditional.  When each team has a list of at least 6-8 questions they select their four favorites.  Each team member

*For more on*
## 3-Step Interview

• Getting to Know You  3: 3
• Guided Grammar  5: 1

writes one question that has not already been written by another team on the chalkboard or butcher paper around the room.

The teacher can make corrections to the questions as they are written in the teams, or as they are put up in front of the class. From the class list of questions, students each select 6 and copy them on a piece of paper with enough space in between to write the answers.

Using a Three-Step Interview format students discover new things about each other, recording the answers on the interview sheet. Answers can be rewritten as a composition about the teammate that can be read as the third step of the activity.

NOTES:

# Turn Toss

Turn Toss is a fun way for students to practice short, predictable vocabulary words and sentence patterns because they are never sure if their turn is coming next. Using a piece of paper wadded up like a snowball, one student gives a prompt and tosses the ball to another who must respond. The second student then tosses it to another and so one following two rules: 1) no send backs - the students must send the ball to a different student than the one who tossed it to them, and 2) change the pattern whenever possible - so that a student never knows for sure if the ball is going to be tossed to them next. If students get distracted with exuberance tossing a wad of paper, just have them slide a pen or pencil across the table to each other instead.

Any list is great content for Turn Toss:
- cardinal numbers
- counting by 2's, 3's, 5's, 10's . . .
  - ordinal numbers
  - days of the week
  - months of the year
  - alphabet

**For more on**

## Turn Toss

## Sample Activities
## Turn Toss:
### Greetings

As students learn to introduce themselves and ask each other's name, use Turn Toss to make practice fun. Have students model the following sentences in rounds until everyone is fluent with the vocabulary. Then combine teams and repeat Turn Toss so that students can practice with new names. For the first week you can combine two different teams each day to begin their class experience with speaking the target language and getting to know each other.
*Round 1:*
What's your name?
*Round 2:*
Hello. My name is _____.
*Round 3:*
Hello, _____. How are you?
*Round 4:*
Fine, thank you. How are you?

## Turn Toss:
### Verb Forms

When it is necessary to look at a particular regular or irregular verb and isolate its forms so that recognize the different conjugations, use Turn Toss. The teacher announces the verb and the first student selects a subject pronoun and tosses the ball to another student. This second student responds with the correct conjugation of the verb, says a different subject pronoun and passes the turn to a third student. The students never know which subject will be chosen or whose turn will be next, so their practice stays lively!

NOTES:

# Who Am I?

Students have a name pinned to their back that they must guess through asking other students questions. Well-known movie stars, cartoon characters, politicians, and characters from literature are good sources.

Make a class list of all the possible names so teams can Roundrobin a list of questions that would help them guess their identity. Put the class list of questions on the overhead projector or chalkboard for easy reference.

## Sample Activities
## Who Am I?:
### Famous Natives
Teams Roundtable a list of famous people who speak the target language and decide which are the four most well-known. Students write the names of the famous people on name tags that will be put on the backs of students in another team.

With their famous person's nametag on their backs, students mill and mingle around the room asking no more than one question of any other student until they guess the name. Limit the number of names and increase the difference in characteristics to simplify the activity.

## Who Am I?:
### Animals
Put pictures of animals whose names are being studied in their vocabulary on the backs of the students. Have a class list of questions on the chalkboard that students can ask to help discover their identities.

## Variation:
## Guess Who:
### Mystery Classmate
Individual students write a description of someone in the class who is not on their team. Teams Roundrobin their compositions and guess who has been written about. Teams can select one composition to be read for the class, or have students take their compositions into an Inside-Outside Circle activity for additional practice. Students are especially motivated to develop listening skills when what is being said may involve them personally.

**For more on**
## Who Am I?

## *Variation:*

# *Where Am I?:*

### Around Town

Using the following vocabulary pictures of common places around town as a reference, teams Roundtable a list of yes/no questions they can ask to determine any of the places indicated. The questions can not name the place specifically. For example, they may ask, "Do you eat here?", or, "Do you read books here?", but not, "Is it the Library?" Since all team members will need a copy of the list of questions, have them all copy the questions, or collect them and photocopy the questions for the students for the next day.

NOTES:

Pass out one vocabulary picture to each student with a paper clip. Have students attach their picture to the back of another student on a different team without showing them the picture. After students have the picture on their back, they mill and mingle about the room asking no more than one of their questions of any other student. When students think they know what the place is on their back, they can stand at the front of the room. After most students think they know "where they are", stop the class and have every student ask another the specific question about where they are.

*Around Town*

*Around Town*

*Around Town*

*Around Town*

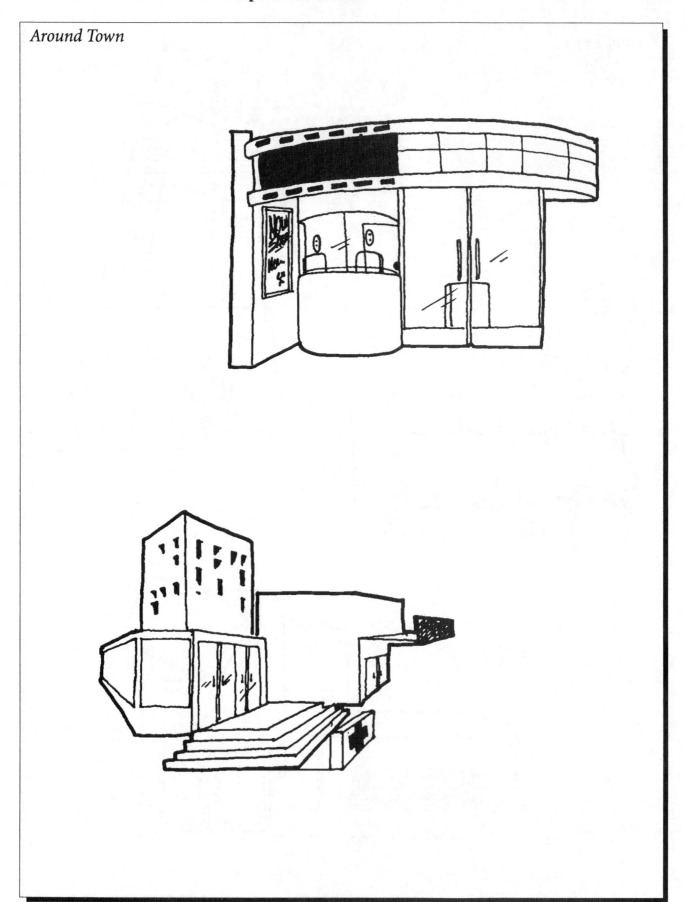

**Julie High:** *Second Language Learning through Cooperative Learning*©
Publisher: Kagan Cooperative Learning • 1 (800) WEE CO-OP

# Social Roles

## Chapter 2

As students transition to interactive lessons they need to develop the cooperative social skills to assume individual responsibility for participating fully. In his book, *Cooperative Learning*, Dr. Spencer Kagan presents a seven-step program, the Structured Natural Approach through which students acquire social skills. For an extensive discussion of the Structured Natural Approach to social skills development, refer to Chapter 14 in *Cooperative Learning*.

## Step 1.
### Set Up a Social Skills Center
Establish a place in the classroom where you can post the Skill-of-the-Week, the Role-of-the-Week, and the gambits associated with the Skill in the target language.

## Step 2.
### Choose a Skill-of-the Week
Select the Skill-of-the Week based on the socialization needs of the students in your class. As students first begin to participate in cooperative learning lessons they will lack many of the skills necessary for success, but you will need to take the time to teach them one at a time for students to eventually acquire them all.

### Step 3. Introduce the Skill-of-the Week
It will be necessary to take a few minutes of class time to identify the Skill-of-the-Week and teach students how to take the Role-of-the-Week.

# Social Skills and Corresponding Social Roles

| Social Skill | Corresponding Role |
|---|---|
| 1. Encouraging Others | *Encourager* |
| 2. Praising Others | *Praiser* |
| 3. Celebrating Accomplishments | *Cheerleader* |
| 4. Equalizing Participation | *Gatekeeper* |
| 5. Helping | *Coach* |
| 6. Asking for Help | *Question Commander* |
| 7. Checking for Understanding | *Checker* |
| 8. Staying on Task | *Taskmaster* |
| 9. Recording Ideas | *Secretary* |
| 10. Reflecting of Group Progress | *Reflector* |
| 11. Not Disturbing Others | *Quiet Captain* |
| 12. Efficiently Distributing Materials | *Materials Monitor* |

*Gatekeeper* — equalizes participation — "Thank you Bill. What's your answer Jose?"

*Praiser* — shows appreciation for contributions — "Great idea!"

*Question Commander* — makes sure students get their questions answered by the team or the teacher if the team doesn't know — "Can anyone answer John's question?

*Coach* — helps other students figure out how to do their work— "Remember to change the verb ending."

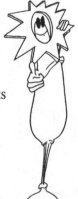

*Encourager* — helps involve everyone — "Let's listen to Juan."

**Taskmaster** — keeps the group on task — "What is the answer to the next question?"

**Materials Monitor** — obtains and returns supplies and makes sure the team cleans up — "Let's put our books away now."

**Secretary** — writes down group answers — "Repeat that slowly, please."

**Cheerleader** — leads the team in a show of group appreciation — "Let's all clap for Mary."

**Reflector** — leads the group in looking back — "How could we do better?"

**Quiet Captain** — makes sure the team does not talk too loudly — "Let's use our 6 inch voices."

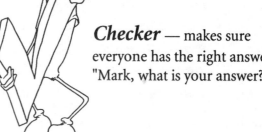

**Checker** — makes sure everyone has the right answer — "Mark, what is your answer?"

### Step 4. Roles and Gambits

Students need to know what to say in a positive tone when assuming the Role-of-the-Week. Give beginning speakers of a second language a few simple phrases to learn for the role. For example, it is the job of the Gatekeeper to make sure there is equal participation in a group. The Gatekeeper needs to learn phrases like, "What do you think, Jose?" and "I would like to hear your idea, Susan." Intermediate and Advanced students can brainstorm unique ways of expressing the role in the target language. Post the phrases on the Social Skills Center bulletin board.

### Step 5. Structures and Structuring

Utilize cooperative learning structures that emphasize development of the Skill-of-the-Week. Reinforce student focus on the content to be mastered as well as the identified social skill.

### Step 6. Model and Reinforce Skill

The teacher takes advantage of every opportunity to model the Skill-of-the-Week for the students. Stop the class and point out to the whole group when the Skill has been applied spontaneously in the classroom. Positive group-based attention is an extremely effective way to establish high expectations for student behavior. For example, you may observe a team that is demonstrating the Skill-of-the-Week and tell the class, "I could barely hear the Gorilla Chasers during that activity because they were using their 6 inch voices so well. Good job, Gorilla Chasers!"

### Step 7. Reflect on Skill

Formally or informally students need to spend some class time reflecting on their experience with the Skill-of-the-Week. Check Spencer Kagan's book, *Cooperative Learning* for a variety of formal reflection form suggestions.

## Structures for Promoting Social Skills*

| Skill | Structures | Chapter |
|---|---|---|
| Listening | Paraphrase Passport | 13 |
| | Three-Step Interview | 12 |
| | Roundrobin | 12 |
| | Two Way Q-Interview | 12 |
| Turn Taking | Roundtable | 8 |
| | Roundrobin | 8 |
| | Team Interview | 12 |
| | Talking Chips | 13 |
| | Turn Toss | 8 |
| Helping | Pairs Check | 10 |
| | Flashcard Game | 10 |
| | Inside-Outside Circle | 10 |
| | Numbered Heads Together | 10 |
| Praising | Pairs Check | 10 |
| | Turn-4-Games | 10, 11 |
| | Affirmation Chips | 13 |
| Polite Waiting | Pairs Check | 10 |

*The chapters referenced refer to Spencer Kagan's book, *Cooperative Learning*, published by Kagan Cooperative Learning.

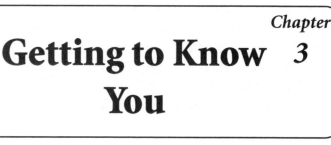

## Chapter 3

# Getting to Know You

Getting to know you is the first chapter of every foreign language/ESL textbook because introducing oneself and meeting new people are among the most common and universal human experiences. The progression of Cooperative Learning structures in this lesson encourages taking advantage of this opportunity to help students feel a sense of belonging in the class as well as develop necessary communication skills.

The activities are organized sequentially according to difficulty. The first day of class with beginning students can include the first few activities. More advanced students can participate in additional activities. As the school year progresses and students gain conversation skills, add more challenging getting acquainted activities into the regular curriculum.

## Structures for
## Getting Acquainted

## *Beginning Getting Acquainted Activities*
## *Inside-Outside Circle:*
### Introductions
Students take turns introducing themselves and greeting each other. Rotate each circle a few times to allow students to master the vocabulary as well as meet most of the class.

## *People Hunt:*
### Find Someone Who...
Students mill and mingle to search for others in the class who have characteristics that match their People Hunt sheet to get their signature next to each description.

## *Roundrobin:*
### Student Introductions
Introduce yourself on the first day of class using only the target language. Have a few of the students demonstrate comprehen-

sion by volunteering to introduce themselves. Choose the team that had the volunteer who performed with the most confidence to model Roundrobin for the class. Each student introduces her/himself going around the team. Have teams pair and repeat the Roundrobin student introductions.

## *Turn Toss:*
### Greetings
As students learn to introduce themselves and ask each other's name, use Turn Toss to make practice fun. Have students model the following sentences in rounds until everyone is fluent with the vocabulary. Then combine teams and repeat Turn Toss so that students can practice with new names. For the first week you can combine two different teams each day to begin their class experience with speaking the target language and getting to know each other.
*Round 1:*
What's your name?
*Round 2:*
Hello. My name is _____.
*Round 3:*
Hello, _____. How are you?
*Round 4:*
Fine, thank you. How are you?

## *Intermediate Getting Acquainted Activities*
## *Guess Who:*
### Mystery Classmate
Individual students write a description of someone in the class who is not on their team. Teams Roundrobin their compositions and guess who has been written about. Teams can select one composition to be read for the class, or have students take their compositions into an Inside-Outside Circle activity for additional practice. Stu-

dents are especially motivated to develop listening skills when what is being said may involve them personally.

## *Roundtable/ Roundrobin:*
### Uncommon Commonalities
Give every team a sheet of blank paper. Have them fold the paper in fourths and draw a rectangle in the middle. Students take turns around the group listing facts about themselves that they write or make a line drawing of on the fourth of the paper closest to them outside of the rectangle.

Teams continue until they discover one unusual fact that all team members share. This fact is then written in the center rectangle as well as in each member's quadrant. Teams can continue the process to see how many uncommon commonalities they share.

## *Advanced Getting Acquainted Activities*
## *4-S Brainstorming:*
### Who Are You?
Students brainstorm questions that they might ask someone they just met and really wanted to get to know. Have one team

# Three-Step Interview:
## Getting To Know You

Have every team member select four questions from the brainstorming list generated in "4-S Brainstorming: Who Are You?" and write them on a separate piece of paper with room for answers. Students pair up and interview each other using their chosen questions. They make notes of the answers to help them paraphrase to the whole team.

# Who Am I?:
## Famous Natives

Teams Roundtable a list of famous people who speak the target language and decide which are the four best known. Students write the names of the famous people on name tags that will be put on the backs of students in another team.

member volunteer to be the recorder. Give the class enough time for each team to generate at least eight questions. Encourage silly questions!

_Beginning People Hunt_

# People Hunt

**Instructions:**

Fill in answers for yourself. Then circulate throughout the class and find another person and ask him/her a question for a match. If you get a yes, sign each other's People Hunt sheets. If you get a no, that person asks you a question looking for a match. Continue alternating asking questions until you find a match, then form new pairs. Try to get all your boxes filled in.

|  | **Signature** |
|---|---|
| 1. Has _____ pets | |
| 2. Has a _____ and a _____ | |
| 3. Gets up at _____ a .m. | |
| 4. Goes to bed at _____ p.m. | |
| 5. Eats _____ | |
| 6. Rides a _____ | |
| 7. Plays _____ | |
| 8. Has a family of _____ | |

_Intermediate People Hunt_

# People Hunt

**Instructions:**
Fill in answers for yourself. Then circulate throughout the class and find another person and ask him/her a question for a match. If you get a yes, sign each other's People Hunt sheets. If you get a no, that person asks you a question looking for a match. Continue alternating asking questions until you find a match, then form new pairs. Try to get all your boxes filled in.

| | **Signature** |
|---|---|
| 1. Has _____ brothers | |
| 2. Favorite class is _____ | |
| 3. _____ before school | |
| 4. Plays _____ on Saturday | |
| 5. Wants to be a _____ | |
| 6. Likes to eat _____ | |
| 7. Is wearing _____ | |
| 8. Has a pet _____ | |

*Advanced People Hunt*

# People Hunt

**Instructions:**

Fill in answers for yourself.  Then circulate throughout the class and find another person and ask him/her a question for a match.  If you get a yes, sign each other's People Hunt sheets.  If you get a no, that person asks you a question looking for a match.  Continue alternating asking questions until you find a match, then form new pairs.  Try to get all your boxes filled in.

| | Signature |
|---|---|
| 1.  Will help you _____ | |
| 2.  Went to the _____ last night | |
| 3.  Likes to go to the _____ | |
| 4.  Has the same favorite _____ as you | |
| 5.  Drives a _____ | |
| 6.  Has the same number of _____ as you | |
| 7.  Would like to visit a _____ | |

# Making Words Mine

## Chapter 4

Learning a second language requires acquisition of extensive, unfamiliar vocabulary. Cooperative Learning structures and activities encourage students to develop vocabulary mastery while they enjoy working together. Foreign language and ESL textbooks often suggest a combination of grammar and vocabulary for every unit. Vocabulary is presented thematically so that many words associated with a particular topic can be learned simultaneously. There are many Cooperative Learning structures that are especially helpful to students for mastering vocabulary.

## Structures for
## Vocabulary Development

- *Flashcard Game* (1: 5)
- *Guess-The-Fib* (1: 7)
- *Inside-Outside Circle* (1: 9)
- *Line-Ups* (1:15)
- *Match Mine* (1:17)
- *Numbered Heads* (1:21)
- *Rallytable* (1:38)
- *Roundrobin* (1:35)
- *Roundtable/Roundrobin* (1:43)
- *Same-Different* (1:47)
- *Send-A-Problem* (1:53)
- *Team Collage* (1:67)
- *Team Draw* (1:68)
- *Where Am I?* (1:78)

## *Sample Activities*
## *Flashcard Game:*
### Vocabulary Review

Breaking down the vocabulary list and making a flashcard for each word students don't know teaches many of the words right away. Have students play the Flashcard Game with every vocabulary list they need to learn.

## *Guess-The-Fib:*
### Vocabulary Fun

**Furniture:** What's in (not in) my house (bedroom, living room, kitchen . . .)?

**Clothing and Colors:** What is s/he wearing (not wearing) today? And who am I talking about?
What's in (not in) my closet?

**Occupations:** What I would (would not) like to be when I grow up.

**Sports and Pastimes:** What I did (did not do) last summer.
What I would like (would not like) to do next summer.

**Around Town:** Where I am going (not going) this week.

**Food & Drink:** Foods I love (hate) to eat.

**Family:** Relatives I am going to (not going to) visit this year.

# Inside-Outside Circle:

## Clothing Vocabulary

Students paste the Clothing vocabulary pictures on one side of a 3 x 5 card and write the name of the item on the other side. In Inside-Outside circles, students quiz each other by first showing the picture side of the card. After their partner says or tries to guess the name of the article of clothing, the students turn the card around and show the correct spelling of the vocabulary word. Have students trade cards before rotating the circle each time. In this way the class can review a large vocabulary list and have a very good time doing it!

# Inside-Outside Circle:

## Flashcard Vocabulary Review

The flashcards created are great for an Inside-Outside Circle. Students should select 3 to 5 of their most challenging vocabulary words. In the Inside-Outside Circles students play Round One of the Flashcard Game, rotate one of the circles and repeat Round One. Then rotate the other circle two times and play the Round Two twice. Make sure that the students can easily see the exaggerated praiser poster so that they include the most important part!

# Line-Ups:

## Poetry Line-Up

To practice a poem or rhyme that the students have already learned to read, cut up the poem into words or lines and give each student one. Students line up according to the order of the poem. When the Line-Up is complete have the class recite the poem together.

When the students have mastered lining up, select a poem that has only a few lines. Cut three or four copies of the poem into lines so that there will be several line-ups.

There will be the additional challenge of students making sure that each line-up is a completed poem. Have the group of students with each particular line of the poem say that line together until the entire poem has been recited.

# Match Mine:

## Everyday Objects & People

Students select individual pictures of Everyday Objects & People vocabulary. Using a piece of notebook paper as a background, students send and receive Match Mine instructions. Students will be additionally practicing preposition vocabulary including above, next to, below, on the left, etc.

# Match Mine:

## My Town

For this Match Mine, the grid is a simple street map with street names typical of a town where the target language is used. The shapes represent buildings and features of a town. One student places two buildings on the map and gives directions to the other student for how to get from one place to the other. Afterwards both students compare maps and building placement. See the following pages.

Another way to use this Match Mine activity is to have one student place several of the shapes on his or her map and simply tell the location for each.

# Roundrobin:

## Days of the Week, Months of the Year, Ordinal Numbers, Cardinal Numbers

Teams recite the designated list of words in a Roundrobin fashion. Different students begin additional rounds so that everyone ends up knowing all the names of the days.

# *Match Mine:* My Town

Variations include:
1. Start the list at a different point.
2. Recite the list backwards.
3. Use a race format — teams recite the list three times in a row and raise their hand when they've finished.
4. Rallyrobin — have students take turns in pairs, each in turn reciting the next item on the list.

# Roundtable/ Roundrobin:

Roundtable/Roundrobin has many applications to vocabulary mastery. Since Roundtable/Roundrobin requires a quick pace to maintain student interest, it is best used to review activities. Recognize speed, improvement in speed and spelling accuracy to generate excitement working together.

# Roundtable/ Roundrobin:

Days and Months
After teaching the days of the week and the months of the year have students Roundtable/Roundrobin the lists. For each round have the student start the list with a different day or month in the sequence. The students can write the lists forward or backward to vary the challenge.

# Roundtable/ Roundrobin:

**Post-Christmas Review**
After Christmas vacation students enjoy Roundtable/Roundrobin as a way to get back into the practice of thinking in the target language. Teams can Roundtable/Roundrobin every word they can think of that begins with a certain letter. Start with easy letters like S, T and R, and proceed with more unusual letters like C, G and L.

Recognize teams who have the longest lists, the most unusual words, the longest words and the shortest words.

One variation of this activity is to have the teams Roundtable/ Roundrobin an alphabetical list of words in the target language. Another variation is to have teams Roundtable/Roundrobin all the words they can think of associated with a particular theme they have studied like Christmas, Clothing, Foods, the House, Parts of the Body, etc.

# Roundtable/ Roundrobin:

**Who's Who?**
Each team receives a different picture showing a variety of vocabulary they are familiar with. Department store catalogs are a good source. Teams Roundtable/Roundrobin descriptions of the picture they have including the illustrated clothing, items included in the setting, any activities they recognize or labels for any of the people pictured. After the descriptions are finished the teacher collects the pictures and mixes them with a few that were not given to any team. All the pictures are placed in front of the class. Teams divide their Roundtable/Roundrobin list so that each member reads part of the description. After each team reads their list the other teams put their heads together to decide which picture has been described. Pictures can be more or less similar to vary difficulty.

# Variation:
# Rallytable:

**Occupations Word Guess**
Referring to the vocabulary pictures for Occupations, students Rallytable a list of yes/no questions that they will ask of the other pair of students on their team to be

able to guess which occupation is pictured inside an envelope. First one student writes a question, then passes the paper to their partner who will say and write another question. When both pairs have prepared a list of at least six questions, they are ready to receive an envelope with a picture of one of the occupations inside. Both pairs of students check to see which picture is included in their envelope, and then they take turns asking their questions until each pair guesses the occupation correctly.

## Same-Different:
### Family

After teaching the vocabulary associated with the names of members of the family, have students do the Same-Different activity located in Chapter 1. They will be practicing the identified words while they enjoy comparing their pictures.

## Same-Different:
### Thematic Vocabulary

Same-Different pictures incorporating thematic vocabulary can be created easily with a copier, a bit of white-out, and a black line pen. Teams can have a list of the current vocabulary available for reference during the Same-Different activity.

## Send-A-Problem:
### Food & Drink

Give each team four of the following Food & Drink vocabulary pictures. Teams simultaneously Roundtable four lists of sentences that describe the item with out saying what it is. Each student writes one sentence for a particular picture and then pass it to the next student until each item has four description sentences. Teams collect and pass in the pictures and share each description with a different other team. Each team should receive four paragraphs.

Each team member reads the description out loud and tries to guess what the food or drink item is. The sending team can verify the answer if there is a question.

## Numbered Heads Together:
### Sports & Pastimes

Make transparencies of the Sports & Pastimes vocabulary pictures. In Step 2 of Numbered Heads, put one of the pictures on the overhead projector. In Step 4 have the designated student from each team go to the chalkboard and write the name of the indicated sport of pastime.

*Variation:* Also indicate a subject pronouns and have the students write a complete sentence about doing the particular sport or pastime.

## Numbered Heads Together:
### Vocabulary Review

Once students know what words are on the current vocabulary list, Numbered Heads is an excellent way for students to practice. The teacher shows an illustration or gives a definition for one of the words. After putting their heads together, teams simultaneously send the designated member to the chalkboard or butcher paper on the wall to write the appropriate word. All correctly spelled words earn points for the team, and the student who writes the word correctly first can earn an additional point to motivate participation.

## Numbered Heads Together:
### What Time Is It?

Telling time can be such a challenge in a foreign language. Simultaneous Numbered

Heads gives the students an opportunity to help each other learn the new phrases while preparing to demonstrate the correct answers to the entire class.

Have a blank clock on the overhead projector or chalkboard. Add the hands to the clock and have students coach each other on how to say and write the correct time. When a number is called every team sends that member to the chalkboard or butcher paper on the wall. Upon a signal from the teacher, they write the appropriate response. When they have all finished writing, have them give the correct answer in a choral response to the question, "What time is it?"

# Team Collage:

## Home Improvement

Teams can use the vocabulary pictures to decorate rooms of a house. Each team receives a large sheet of paper and a different color of marker pen for every team member. Each team member can only use the marker they select as they draw together an outline of a house with rooms that they can decorate with the vocabulary pictures. Each team member selects three of the following pictures that they will place on the house collage. If the students want to decorate the pictures, they will need to cooperate in asking each other to apply each of the available marker colors. Once they have place the pictures, teams Roundtable a description of their house. Each team member contributes one sentence at a time until there are at least three sentences per student included in the description. Teams stand to show their collage and each student reads an equal number of sentences in the description. Have the teams post their houses on the classroom wall until the next vocabulary unit.

# Team Draw:

## Team Dream Home

After vocabulary associated with the house is presented, teams create a dream home with rooms, furniture and architecture that all members agree would be a special place to live.

## Variation:

# Where Am I?:

## Around Town

Using the vocabulary pictures of common places around town as a reference, teams Roundtable a list of yes/no questions they can ask to determine any of the places indicated. The questions cannot name the place specifically. For example, they may ask, "Do you eat here?", or, "Do you read books here?", but not, "Is it the Library?" Since all team members will need a copy of the list of questions, have them all copy the questions, or collect them and photocopy the questions for the students for the next day.

Pass out one vocabulary picture to each student with a paper clip. Have students attach their picture to the back of another student on a different team without showing them the picture. After students have the picture on their back, they mill and mingle about the room asking no more than one of their questions of any other student. When students think they know what the place is on their back, they can stand at the front of the room. After most students think they know "where they are", stop the class and have every student ask another the specific question about where they are.

In the communicative approach to teaching foreign language grammar, structures are always introduced and practiced in the context of negotiating meaning. Guided Grammar Experiences include meaningful communication and are integrated with the essential thematic vocabulary of the lesson. The teacher's challenge is to create opportunities for repeated practice with grammar structures that motivate participation and communication while encouraging mastery.

Cooperative Learning structures allow students to use the target language to talk about what they enjoy most — themselves. Grammar practice activities that incorporate personal themes and give students the chance to ask each other questions about mechanics accelerate learning of the structures and contribute to a positive experience while mastering a second language.

### Structures for
## Guided Grammar
## Experiences

- **Flashcard Game** (1: 5)
- **Numbered Heads** (1:21)
- **Pairs Check** (1:27)
- **Roundtable** (1:37)
- **Roundtable/Roundrobin** (1:43)
- **Send-A-Problem** (1:53)
- **Three-Step Interview** (1:73)
- **Turn Toss** (1:75)

## *Sample Activities*
## *Three-Step*
## *Interview*
### New Grammar Practice

As students learn new tenses Three-Step Interview is an excellent way to give them practice with the new verb structures. Teams first Roundtable/ Roundrobin questions they would like to ask each other within the newly introduced time reference: present, past, future, conditional. When each team has a list of at least 6-8 questions they select their four favorites. Each team member writes one question on the chalkboard or butcher paper around the room that question has not already been written by another team.

The teacher can make corrections to the questions as they are written in the teams, or as they are put up in front of the class. From the class list of posted questions, students each select 6 and copy them on a piece of paper with enough space in between to write the answers.

Using a Three-Step Interview format students discover new things about each other, recording the answers on the interview sheet. Answers can be rewritten as a composition about the teammate that can be read as the third step of the activity.

# Flashcard Game:

## Grammar Practice

Playing the Flashcard Game with grammar content can help students when memorization is required. Students can make flashcards to study:

- Irregular verb forms
- Subject/verb agreement with regular and irregular verbs
- Verb ending transformation for various tenses.

Care must be taken to incorporate the grammar forms acquired into meaningful opportunities to communicate.

# Pairs Check:

## Guided Grammar Practice

Assign part or all of a grammar practice activity from the textbook or teacher-made worksheet that will give students the opportunity to demonstrate understanding of a new grammatical structure. Model the guided practice activity for the class to make sure all students understand what is required. Pairs of students do the grammar exercise, checking with the other pair on the team after every two items.

# Roundtable:

## Alphabetical Parts of Speech

Parts of speech lend themselves to the pace of the Roundtable format. Teams Roundtable nouns, verbs or adverbs beginning with each letter of the alphabet. For a variation, reverse the order of the alphabet or start with a different letter than "A."

# Roundtable/ Roundrobin:

## Grammar Practice

When learning to conjugate verbs, Roundtable/Roundrobin is an especially good way to check for understanding. The teacher uses the direct instruction in particular verbs and then gives an unfamiliar example for students to Roundtable/ Roundrobin. By circulating around the room while the teams help each other with the forms, the teacher can assess comprehension and address individual questions while the entire class is actively involved in guided practice.

Roundtable/Roundrobin with verb conjugations is also a good way to begin class with a brief, involving activity that helps students transition into thinking in the target language.

# Roundtable/ Roundrobin:

## What's Going On?

Each team receives a fairly detailed picture with many activities depicted. Teams Roundtable/Roundrobin a list of all nouns, verbs, and/or adjectives illustrated. More

advanced students can then Roundtable/ Roundrobin a story about the picture using their previous lists to begin sentences.

# Roundtable/Roundrobin:

## In a Hurry! (Reflexive Verbs)

Students imagine that they have been at the beach all day and only have a few minutes to get ready to go to a party. They Roundtable/Roundrobin all the necessary activities that must be completed before they are ready.

# Send-A-Problem:

## Grammar Practice

At the point in the grammar lesson where the class needs guided practice, assign a few key items from a textbook or teacher-made worksheet. You many want to use the Pairs Check structure to formalize students helping each other with the exercise. When the students have demonstrated that they can do the provided exercise with confidence, have them create their own sample exercises following the model given using the Send-A-Problem structure. Be sure to monitor student participation to check correctness and assist with clarification.

# Numbered Heads Together:

## Grammar Review

Reviewing verb forms and grammatical structures before a test is best done in a Simultaneous Numbered Heads format. To review verb forms the teacher gives the infinitive form of the verb first and then designates the subject. With their heads together students rehearse the answer. After a number is called, that student from every team goes to the chalkboard or butcher paper around the room. Upon the teacher's signal, they write their answer. Teams earn a recognition point for the correct answer as well as a bonus point for the team who put the correct answer up first.

# Pairs Check:

## Homework Check

Students can use the Pairs Check structure to discuss their homework efforts before the bell rings and during the first five minutes of class. If there are not four students with their completed assignment in a particular team, they can check their work in Step 7 with a pair from another team.

# Turn Toss:

## Verb Forms

When it is necessary to look at a particular regular or irregular verb and isolate its forms so that recognize the different conjugations, use Turn Toss. The teacher announces the verb and the first student selects a subject pronoun and tosses the ball to another student. This second student responds with the correct conjugation of the verb, says a different subject pronoun and passes the turn to a third student. The students never know which subject will be chosen or whose turn will be next, so their practice stays lively!

# Writing Skills

Secondary students especially need to practice writing the words they are learning to use in oral communication. Writing activities need to give students opportunities to manipulate written language that corresponds to what they are hearing modeled and learning to use in conversation.

## *Sample Activities*

## *4-S Brainstorming:*

### Original Invention

Teams send a representative to the front of the class to blindly choose an item out of a shopping bag that the teacher holds. The bag contains some of the oddities from a kitchen gadget drawer, such as a melon baller, lemon wedge squeezer, garlic press, whisk, ice cream scoop, tea ball, or egg yolk strainer. Teams brainstorm unusual uses for the item using the 4-S Brainstorming structure.

Once a long list of unusual uses has been generated in every team, teams select their use to create a T.V. advertisement to present to the class. The advertisement can include innovative packaging of the item, demonstrations for its use, a jingle that will help it sell, as well as a dynamic poster to motivate the consumer. This activity generates a lot of laughter as well as vocabulary expansion. Videos of the team presentations make interesting viewing for the class.

## *Line-Ups:*

### Sentence Building Line-Up

Students stand in team clusters around the room. Each team is given a group of cards with subject, verb, adjective, and noun cards taken from the vocabulary being studied by the class. The team members select cards that make a sentence. Each student hides their card until it is their team's turn to present their sentence. All together the students on a team turn their cards so that the other teams in the class can read their sentence. Put a rule in place that no team can repeat a sentence already presented by another. There may be some last minute scrambling!

## *Pairs Check:*

### Homework Check

Students can use the Pairs Check structure to discuss their homework efforts before

---

### Structures for
# Writing Skills

---

the bell rings and during the first five minutes of class. If there are not four students with their completed assignment in a particular team, they can check their work in Step 7 with a pair from another team.

# Roundtable/ Roundrobin:

## After the Movie

After students see a film in the target language they can work in teams to create presentations that will clarify and demonstrate their understanding of the content. Using a Roundtable/Roundrobin structure, teams write their own version of:

- What might happen to the main character in 5 years.
- The dialogue at a particularly important part of the story.
- An alternate ending.

Team presentations can imitate or parody what they saw in the film.

# Roundtable/ Roundrobin:

## Dialogue

Show pictures of interesting-looking natives from a country where the target language is spoken and explain that they are going to have a conversation. Teams create a dialogue using a Roundtable/ Roundrobin format by first answering the questions: Who?, What?, When?, Where?, and Why? They proceed to write a script of a minimum number of verbal exchanges between the characters. There should be one character for each member of the team. Current topics of study in vocabulary and grammatical structures can be designated by the teacher to be included in the dialogue. Teams can present their dialogues using costumes and props.

# Roundtable/ Roundrobin:

## Happy Endings

Students read a short story appropriate to their ability level from which the ending has been omitted. Teams Roundtable/ Roundrobin the final paragraph(s) and present their ending to the class. Encourage use of props, humor and dramatic flair. Since every team has the same story to start with, they will be familiar with the context and vocabulary applied to the variety of endings.

# Simultaneous Roundtable/ Roundrobin:

## Stop Story

Give every team a copy of an interesting picture. In Simultaneous Roundtable fashion every student on the team starts to write their own story about the picture. After three minutes the teacher calls "stop,"

and students take their pen off the paper at whatever point in the sentence. The stories are rotated to the next team member who has a chance to read what has been started and then three more minutes to add another part. After every student has contributed at least once to each story, the teams Roundrobin all four stories. The best of the four can be selected and presented to the class in a simple reading, or as a skit with props and costumes.

# Story Scramble:
## Cultural Selection

Foreign language and ESL textbooks usually include brief sections that address interesting cultural differences in countries where the target language is spoken. Make a copy of one of the articles for each team and use the Story Scramble structure. After the teams have discussed the correct order of the article, focus their attention on the original source so they can see the article printed in its entirety.

# Story Scramble:
## Poetry

Find poems in the target language that have four to twelve lines to cut up into strips. Let teams suggest alternate ways to structure the poem.

# Lesson Designs

In this last section of the book, we examine two cooperative learning lesson designs particularly helpful to promote language acquisition. The difference between a lesson design and a structure is that a lesson is a broader framework, extends over a longer time period, and can contain a number of structures

After your classes have learned various cooperative learning structures and used them several times, it is possible to design extended lessons that incorporate a series of different structures. These extended lessons can span several hours of class time, concluding with a culminating group project that is presented to the class.

## Structures for
# Lesson Designs

- *Flashcard Game*  (1: 5)
- *Gallery Tour*  (1:59)
- *Proactive Prioritizing*  (1:31)
- *Roam the Room*  (1:60)
- *Roundtable/Roundrobin*  (1:43)
- *Spend-A-Buck*  (1:63)
- *Two Stay, Two Stray* (1:60)
- *Team Collage*  (1:67)
- *Team Discussion*

## Lesson Design 1
# Co-op Co-op

The 10 steps of Co-op Co-op are described in detail in Spencer Kagan's book, *Cooperative Learning*. The design allows individual and team creativity on a topic of general interest to the entire class.

### Step 1: Student-Centered Class Discussion
Students contribute to a class list of suggestions for discovery in the unit. You may wish to use a Simultaneous Blackboard Share as students from each team come up to add to the class list.

### Step 2: Selection of Student Learning Teams
This is an opportunity to vary team formation, if desired. It may be more appropriate for students to work in their established heterogeneous teams. However, it is possible for students to be recombined according to their interest in the Co-op Co-op topic.

### Step 3: Teambuilding and Cooperative Skill Development
If new teams are formed, it will be important to take enough time for the Teambuilding necessary for students to feel comfortable working together. Depending on the social skill needs of the class, certain roles can be introduced along with their

gambits in the target language that students can use to facilitate their group process.

### Step 4: Team Topic Selection
If new teams were not created around interest in the list of topics generated in Step 1, teams now select which topic they will pursue. No topic can be researched by more than one team. Each team can use their topic as the title of a poster that goes on the classroom wall so the class can appreciate all of the aspects of general interest that will be covered.

Evaluation criteria for team presentations need to be discussed in detail at this point so that the teams have them in mind as they begin thinking about their presentations. You may wish to use Proactive Prioritizing as students select their Team Topics.

### Step 5: Minitopic Selection
Just as every team selects a unique topic to study, every team member selects one aspect of that topic for his or her individual contribution which will be unique and discernible when the team makes its presentation. The teacher and all team members need to agree to the minitopic selections. Some thought to the final presentation can help team members decide what particular aspects need to be addressed as minitopics.

Evaluation criteria for minitopic presentations need to be discussed in detail at this point so that students will be able to have them in mind as they begin thinking about their presentations.

### Step 6: Minitopic Preparation
Students prepare their minitopics individually, but class time to discuss and create their contributions together will facilitate cohesive team presentations. Every stu-

dent is responsible for a visual display as well as some written product.

### Step 7: Minitopic Presentations
Minitopic presentations are formal opportunities for teammates to appreciate the work each team member has done individually. Afterwards, teams will design the team presentation that will be exhibited for the class. Minitopic Presentations provide a natural opportunity for evaluation of individual effort. Suggested Structure: Roundrobin.

### Step 8: Preparation of Team Presentations
The team responsibility at this point is to design a presentation that is not simply a sequential exhibition of the minitopic presentations, but a synthesis through which each team member participates in the demonstration of the overall understanding of the Team Topic. The teacher can help with encouragement of creative and enterprising approaches to the presentations.

### Step 9: Team Presentations
Follow each team presentation with a question/answer period where each other team observing is required to pose three questions. You may wish to use a Team Inside-

Outside Circle for team presentations. Each team presents to another team rather than the whole class.

## Step 10: Evaluation

Evaluation takes place on three levels:
- Team presentations are evaluated by the class.
- Individual contributions to the team effort are evaluated by teammates.
- Minitopic presentations are evaluated by the teacher and in Step 7.

Evaluation criteria needs to be shared with the students as they begin planning their presentations.

### Sample Co-op Co-op Lesson 1

# Co-op Co-op:
## At the Mall

In this Co-op Co-op lesson design teams select a type of store found in a mall, so that when all teams present simultaneously the classroom will simulate a mall. Vocabulary associated with various topics will be explored, including clothing, animals, food, beauty, etc. This is an excellent opportunity to introduce the foreign currency system and any cultural differences in the conventions of shopping and ordering food in a restaurant. On the day of the team presentations, students will participate as shop owners and as shoppers at each other's stores. Teams will be evaluated according to the authenticity of their simulations. Individual contributions should be discernible. Every student will turn in a worksheet showing what they bought during the simulation.

## Step 1: Student-Centered Class Discussion
# Roundtable/ Roundrobin:
### Kinds of Stores

Teams Roundtable/Roundrobin all the kinds of stores they have ever seen at a mall

**Steps 2-3:** Refer to pages 7: 1 and 7: 2.

## Step 4: Team Topic Selection
# Spend-A-Buck:
### Choose a Store

If students are to remain in their ongoing heterogeneous teams for the Co-op Co-op unit, Spend-A-Buck is a good way to prioritize preferences and decide which store teams want to simulate. Using the Spend-A-Buck structure, teams identify which store they will create together for the mall simulation. As soon as they have chosen a type of store, each team writes their selection on the chalkboard so there is no duplication.

*Step 5: Minitopic Selection*
# Roundtable/ Roundrobin:
## What's in Store?

Teams Roundtable/Roundrobin everything they might see if they went into their particular kind of store at a mall. Teams then identify any categories that link items on the list. Students can choose minitopics from these categories. Responsibility for minitopic presentation can include providing the props, costumes and advertising posters that will distinguish their store. Students can script possible interactions with customers so they are prepared to respond.

*Steps 6-8:* Refer to page 7: 2.

*Step 9: Team Presentations*
# Two Stay, Two Stray:
## Shopping Day

During the simulations, two members of the team stay with the store to deal with the customers. Every team needs to prepare

facsimiles of foreign currency in advance so that each member will have money to go shopping, and every store will have money to make change. Items for sale each have a 3x5 card in front giving the name of the item. No prices are advertised so that shoppers must ask for the price of the item. Every student must buy at least one thing from three stores. They write on a piece of paper what they bought, the price and the reason they bought it. Students do not remove their purchases from the store. Shop owners keep track of what items have sold. When half the class period is over, shoppers and shop owners switch roles and the process is repeated.

*Sample Co-op Co-op Lesson 2*
# Co-op Co-op:
## World Tour Simulation

*Step 1: Student-Centered Class Discussion*
# Roundtable/ Roundrobin:
## Where in the World?

Locate a one-page world map with the countries highlighted where the target language is spoken. Many foreign language textbooks have a map like this at the beginning of the book. Copy the map without names of the countries so that students can try to think of them.

Teams Roundtable/Roundrobin the map helping each other label as many of the countries' names as they can think of together. When all teams have completed as many as they can, show a regular world map so they can fill in the rest of the names.

# *Roundrobin:*
## World Facts
Team members tell anything they know about any of these countries, one fact at a time, using the Roundrobin structure.

## Step 4: Team Topic Selection
# *Proactive Prioritizing:*
## Favorite Country
Looking at the completed world map with the countries highlighted where the target language is spoken, teams select the 5 countries they would most like to know more about. In a Roundrobin format students make positive statements of interest in particular countries such as: "I would like to know what the food is like in Guatemala," or "I want to know what the weather is like in Tibet." Rotate around the teams several times.

"Chile is on the west coast of South America."

Have each team determine which one country they would like to study in depth together. When a team has selected its country, one team member lists their team name and the name of the country on a large piece of butcher paper or chart paper. Only one team can sign up to research any particular country, so the first team to make a particular choice has priority.

## Step 5: Minitopic Selection
# *Roundtable/ Roundrobin:*
## Need to Know
Students imagine that they have been hired to direct the office of tourism for the country they have selected. Teams Roundtable/ Roundrobin all the aspects of a country that they would need to learn about. The list might include food, sports, native costumes, music, dances, art, literature, famous people, and government.

Each student selects the one area of most interest to him or her. Only one student may work on any particular aspect. They need to know that they will be responsible for creating some type of demonstration to illustrate the area they choose.

## Step 6: Minitopic Preparation
# *Team Collage:*
## Our Country
Students gather information on their topic from travel books, encyclopedias, foreign consulates, magazines, interviews with people who have lived in their chosen country, and interviews with teachers. Each student brings a selection of materials to class to create a team poster about the country. Encourage students to bring various pictures and small items other than pictures to mount on their posters. The poster can show the four distinct areas of

study in the corners. As the pictures show elements that connect more than one area, they can be placed more towards the center of the poster.

# Roam the Room:
## Take A Look
At the beginning of the following class period, students move around the room as individuals to view the posters made by other teams. After a few minutes teams assemble and Roundtable/ Roundrobin to share positive statements about what they have seen. The most positive statement about each poster is written on a separate piece of paper. When all teams have finished, the compliments are delivered to the other teams.

## Step 7: Minitopic Presentations
# Roundrobin:
### Minitopic Presentation
Minitopic Presentations need to include some type of demonstration. The aspects of dances, food, costumes, music and art are more easily demonstrated than government or weather, but students can make an individual poster to accompany their Mini-Topic Presentation.

## Step 8: Preparation of Team Presentations
# Team Discussion:
### Presentation Planning
After their Minitopic Presentations, teams need to decide how they will make their Team Presentation. The team decides the order for the demonstrations that will be repeated for the whole class, and also plan an additional whole team activity that connects the four parts of their presentation.

Teams write four questions for the rest of the class to answer as they watch the presentation.

## Step 9: Team Presentations
# Gallery Tour:
### 'Round the World
Team Presentations may take more than one day depending on the degree to which teams have prepared interesting and informative exhibitions. If the presentations are all going to be something very special, it may be preferable to take the time to have teams present one at a time to the entire class. Otherwise the Gallery Tour structure saves class time and provides a unique possibility for an exciting learning activity. Divide the class in half by asking for teams to volunteer to do their presentations.

On a designated day the first half of the teams will present while the other half tours the exhibitions. The touring students have the questions prepared by the other teams to answer when they visit their presentation. When students come dressed in costume, provide ethnic foods, play regional music and speak in the target language it will seem like the class is at a foreign bazaar. Either the next day or the next week have the teams switch roles. Be sure to invite parents, the principal, other teachers, school board members, and local politicians if the class is willing.

*Lesson Design 2*

# Color-Coded Co-op Cards

Color-Coded Co-op Cards are a great way to structure memory work. Students enjoy the Flashcard Game they play with the Color-Coded Co-op Cards and memorizing seems more like fun.

There are ten steps to Color-Coded Co-op Cards:

### Step 1: Pretest

Vocabulary should be presented to students in context with dialogue, pictures, filmstrips, audio tapes or realia. In this way students often learn a few of the required words right away. In the pretest step of Color-Coded Co-op Cards students have the opportunity to assess their own needs for mastering the vocabulary list. The pretest should be simple. Show students the pictures, filmstrip frames or realia used to introduce the vocabulary and have them write the words. Since at this point they won't know the entire list, tell the students to try to visualize the word and write whatever part of the word they can remember. This activity helps them to create the memory pattern for the correct spelling.

### Step 2: Students Create Color-Coded Co-op Cards

Each student on the team makes a set of flashcards for the vocabulary s/he missed. Every student on a team uses a different color paper so that they can easily identify their flashcards. The cue side of the card should be a picture or drawing (not the word in the student's primary language!). The textbook often provides simple line drawings that can be copied.

### Step 3: Students play the Flashcard Game (2 Rounds)

To play the Flashcard Game all students will need to know how to say exaggerated praisers in the target language. "Is your name Einstein?" or "You sure are a genius!" surprise and delight students who learn their vocabulary list all the faster for the encouragement and fun. Create a class list of exaggerated praisers for a poster that can go on the classroom wall for students to refer to for the Flashcard Game and other times as well. The list must be fairly long so that tutors will not have to repeat any praiser during a round of the Flashcard Game. When you hear any student make up a new exaggerated praiser during the game, stop the class and recognize that student for her/his imagination. Have the student write the new praiser on the class poster. This group-based positive attention will start all the students trying to think of more creative ways of encouraging each other. This really adds to their enthusiasm for learning vocabulary!

*Round 1: Maximum Cues*

Students pair up and decide who will be the tutor first. The tutees give their cards to the tutors who proceed holding up one card at a time, first showing the front of the card with the cue and then turning the card and saying the answer to the tutees. The tutors then turn the card around again, showing the front, and the tutees try to give the answer. If the answer is correct, the tutor gives an exaggerated praise and the tutee earns the return of the flash card. If the tutee does not give a correct response s/he is entitled to a "helper" rather than a "praiser". Helpers are hints of any kind including showing the back of the card again. If a helper is given, the flashcard is not won back but placed at the bottom of the stack of cards to practice again.

When the tutee has won back all of his or her cards, the tutor and tutee switch roles.

*Round 2: Few Cues*
After both students have played Round 1, they progress to Round 2. The game is played in the same way except that with fewer cues the students move from short to long-term memory. The tutors show the front of the card only, and the tutees try to remember the back. Exaggerated praisers or helpers follow every attempt.

### Step 4: Practice Test
A practice test shows the students what they have learned as well as what still needs to be mastered.

### Step 5: Initial Color-Coded Improvement Scoring
Team members mark every flashcard that they spelled correctly on the practice test with a star and pile them in the middle of their table. The total number is the improvement score for the team. The teams can report this number to the class and be celebrated along with the class total.

### Step 6: Repeated practice on missed items
Repeat the Flashcard Game with any remaining cards.

### Steps 7 & 8: Final Test & Final Improvement Scoring
Students take the final test and a team improvement score is calculated by having students count their correct cards. If the entire process of doing Color-Coded Co-op Cards spans a few days with other activities mixed in, some students will need incentive to help them keep track of their flash cards so that they have them to as a study aid for the final test. Teams in which every member has all their cards on the day of the final test could receive extra points to add to the class goal thermometer.

### Step 9: Individual, Team and Class Recognition
Success is celebrated at three levels:
1. Individuals post their improvement scores on a graph they keep, and all students who improved more this week than last stand up and take a bow as they are recognized by the class.
2. Teams announce their total improvement scores which are posted on a class thermometer with a marker pen in their team color.
3. The class appreciates the progress they have made toward a class goal represented by achieving a certain level on the thermometer.

### Step 10: Processing
Students discuss the effect of using the Color-Coded Co-op Cards to learn the vocabulary list. They also discuss any suggestions for improving the process to increase their success.

## *Sample Activities*
# 𝒥lashcard 𝒢ame:
### Vocabulary Review
Color-Coded Co-op Cards are a fun way to memorize vocabulary by breaking down the vocabulary list and making a flashcard for each word students don't know, they learn many of the words right away. Use Color-Coded Co-op Cards and have students play the Flashcard Game with every vocabulary list they need to memorize.

## *Flashcard Game:*
### Learning Foods

Using a magazine with many pictures of food, students make their flashcards with pictures on one side and the vocabulary word on the other side. Allow them to select a few pictures of food vocabulary that are not identified in the text, but interest them individually. As they play the Flashcard Game, they will learn new words from each other's unique choices as well as review textbook vocabulary.

## *Flashcard Game:*
### Irregular Verb Mastery

Have students play the Flashcard Game when they are learning difficult or irregular verb forms. They should put the infinitive form on one side of the flashcards with the challenging subject pronoun written below it. On the answer side of the flashcard students write the subject pronoun first and the correct conjugation following it. See samples below.

*Sample Co-op Cards for irregular verbs:*

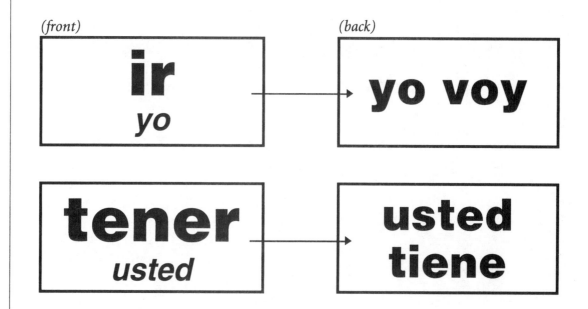

**Curran, Lorna.** *Cooperative Learning Lessons for Little Ones: Literature-based Language Arts and Social Skills.* San Juan Capistrano, CA: Kagan Cooperative Learning, 1990.

**Kagan, Spencer.** *Cooperative Learning.* San Juan Capistrano, CA: Kagan Cooperative Learning, 1992.

**Kagan, Spencer.** *Same Different, Holidays Edition.* San Juan Capistrano, CA: Kagan Cooperative Learning, 1991.

**Krashen, Stephen D. and Terrell, Tracy D.** *The Natural Approach to Language Acquisition in the Classroom.* California, Alemany Press, 1983.

**Gaies, Stephen J.** *Peer Involvement in Language Learning.* Prentice Hall Regents, New Jersey, 1985.

**Robertson, Laurie, & Rodriguez, Celso.** *Match Mine.* San Juan Capistrano, CA: Kagan Cooperative Learning, 1991.

**Stone, Jeanne.** *Cooperative Learning and Language Arts: A Multi-Structural Approach.* San Juan Capistrano, CA: Kagan Cooperative Learning, 1989.

**Wiederhold, Chuck.** *Cooperative Learning and Higher Level Thinking: The Q-Matrix.* San Juan Capistrano, CA: Kagan Cooperative Learning, 1991.

## Chapter 9

# About the Author
## Julie High

Hello! I am Julie High. I am very proud that this book has been published by *Kagan Cooperative Learning*. As a high school French teacher for twelve years, and an ESL teacher for five years, my students enjoyed so much greater success with the Structural Approach to Cooperative Learning that it is a pleasure to share our experiences with you through these chapters.

I became fascinated with the language acquisition process in high school, and enjoy developing trilingual proficiency in Spanish, French and English. As a Title VII Project Director for North Monterey County Unified School District in California, I have been able to see the remarkable changes for Limited English Proficient middle school and elementary students whose teachers begin using the structures as a vehicle for presenting, reviewing and extending content learning.

I love animals, kids, and teaching, and seem to be involved with one or another at just about every moment of the day. When I am not at work, which sometimes seems the exception, I am at home playing with my dog or riding my horse.

If you have any questions about the material in this book I would be glad to hear from you. Address any mail to me in care of *Kagan Cooperative Learning*, 27134 Paseo Espada, Suite 303, San Juan Capistrano, CA 92675. Until we meet, ¡Hasta luego!